Sonoma County Wine Library

Wine, Food, & the Good Life

Wine, Food, & the Good Life

RECIPES CELEBRATING 50 YEARS OF FAMILY WINEMAKING

Arlene Mueller

Dorothy Indelicato

PUBLISHED BY WINE APPRECIATION GUILD

Other books published by The Wine Appreciation Guild:

WINE LOVERS' COOKBOOK
THE CHAMPAGNE COOKBOOK
EPICUREAN RECIPES OF CALIFORNIA WINEMAKERS
GOURMET WINE COOKING THE EASY WAY
FAVORITE RECIPES OF CALIFORNIA WINEMAKERS
DINNER MENUS WITH WINE
EASY RECIPES OF CALIFORNIA WINEMAKERS
THE POCKET ENCYCLOPEDIA OF CALIFORNIA WINE
IN CELEBRATION OF WINE AND LIFE
WINE CELLAR RECORD BOOK
CORKSCREWS: Keys to Hidden Pleasures
THE CALIFORNIA WINE DRINK BOOK
THE CALIFORNIA BRANDY DRINK BOOK
NEW ADVENTURES IN WINE COOKERY
WINE IN EVERYDAY COOKING
THE WINE LOVERS' COOKBOOK

THE VINTAGE IMAGE SERIES:

THE NAPA VALLEY TOUR BOOK
THE NAPA VALLEY WINE BOOK
THE SONOMA MENDOCINO TOUR BOOK
THE SONOMA MENDOCINO WINE BOOK
THE CENTRAL COAST TOUR BOOK
THE CENTRAL COAST WINE BOOK

Published by:

THE WINE APPRECIATION GUILD Ltd.
155 Connecticut Street
San Francisco, CA 94107

(415) 864-1202

Library of Congress Catalog Number: 85-051575

ISBN: 0-932664-47-4

Editors: Donna Bottrell, Maurice Sullivan
Book Design: Ronna Nelson

Table of Contents

A Time To Celebrate

Wine has always been an intricate part of our family tradition. We consider wine a food and a necessary part of our daily meal, a part of our family social structure. Never were we denied wine in either my husband's family or my family as we were growing up. Therefore there was no strong desire to overindulge. Wine is a food and that is how wine is to be consumed; nothing more, nothing less. Our parents were always there as role models showing us how to appreciate wine with food. We were taught how to enjoy wine and how to respect it for all its good qualities. We have in turn taught our children the same values.

Compiling the recipes and family history has been work, but fun also. We've learned how difficult it is to measure ingredients. All these years we've been using a handful of this and a pinch of that. That's how Mom does it. We didn't realize how difficult it is to put a "handful of this" down on paper. How easy it is when someone is standing next to you and you can literally show them "how much" and how the end product should taste. Writing the instructions down on paper is an entirely different story. It took several revisions of the recipe instructions because of misinterpretations. For instance, when we were trying to tell Arlene how we make Filozes, we said, gesturing with our hands, "Do it like this." She nodded "yes" but until we actually did the recipe with her watching, we weren't able to get the proper words on paper. (Arlene and I have put on an extra ten pounds of weight but we've enjoyed the project.)

The gathering of the recipes in this cookbook has given us many rewards. We've rekindled old friendships and have made some new ones. Some recipes that may have been lost will now be saved for the future generations. We experimented with the old recipes and improved upon some of them. By publishing this cookbook, we've piqued the interest in cooking the old recipes by the younger relatives. We feel confident our family traditions will at least survive another generation.

Papa, circa 1912.

We've also noticed the rippling effect it's had on the friends and relatives we've asked to critique our recipes. They are beginning to recognize how important tradition is to them as a family. This caused them to investigate their own family food treasures.

It is our plan to continue collecting family recipes. We've become so much more aware of the foods family members prepare that we have long taken for granted. I've taken to observing and writing those observations down before all is lost.

Collecting stories for the history portion of the book allowed my mind to search back: I can remember as a youngster my mother telling me when she was only nine years old how she literally stomped grapes for her father. He was a Portuguese immigrant newly in the United States from the island of St. Michael, Azores Islands and he didn't have any of the equipment that is available today. She learned the old country ways of making wine with her feet. Part of my grandfather's wine cellar is in our home wine cellar today. My grandmother gave me Grandpa's old spigot that he used in the 1920 era to remove the wine from the barrels. I have it framed on the wall of our wine cellar at home. I can remember how my grandmother, as she got along in years, always had a glass of port before retiring in the evening. Her doctor had recommended this "remedy" in lieu of pills. She said the doctor said she needed to improve the quality of her blood and that she needed to relax before she went to bed. We saw to it that Grandma always had plenty of "medication."

As we collected the 50 years of family history, we learned many new stories. Not all of us knew that my father-in-law in his younger days delivered 50 gallons of wine off the truck to customers; 50 gallons plus a 100 pound barrel! That's over 500 pounds. In his zeal to feed his growing family, he would deliver the wine day after day, putting this difficult strain on his body. He was a stocky, muscular man, but this heavy burden took its toll in his later years. I can remember how carefully he walked. He was silently enduring the back pain that was a result of his need to feed and clothe his family. I remember him as a kind, gentle man that my children loved dearly. We have many happy memories that we all love to share with anyone who will listen.

I'm looking forward to meeting many new people as a result of this book. I'm hoping that after you've tried some of our recipes you'll stop in our Tasting Room and say "Hello." I'm hoping you'll say, "I tried this recipe and I like it very much," or "I tried this variation and I like it better; would you like to try my version?"

By collecting the 50 years of family history and recipes, we've enriched our lives many times over. We hope that, in some small way, we can enrich your family's traditions by copying some of our good times. We know that family, food and wine is the way to the Good Life.

—Dorothy Indelicato

Dorothy Indelicato

Dorthy Cardoza Indelicato spent her childhood within sight of the vineyards. Later, she married Vincent Indelicato, Executive Vice President of the winery. Today, in addition to her duties as Treasurer of Delicato Vineyards, she manages the winery's tasting room and gift shop. At home, she prepares dishes from her husband's Italian heritage as well as recipes from her own family's Portuguese background. Her interest in preserving the Indelicato traditions and winemaking history is evident throughout this book.

Cooking With Wine

This cookbook puts the good life within your reach. It shows how to prepare delicious, wholesome foods at moderate cost without spending all day in the kitchen. The recipes that follow feature nutritious ingredients, convenient preparation, and the good taste that comes from cooking with wine.

Good health is essential to the good life. Vegetables and fruits account for 34 recipes. The book offers more than 17 distinctly different poultry recipes plus plenty of good fish dishes. Frying and sautéeing are kept to a minimum.

We advise "salt and pepper to taste," but have tested the recipes using little or no salt. Because wine adds natural flavor to a dish, you'll find that salt usually can be reduced or omitted.

Fresh ingredients are crucial. Buy what's in season for maximum flavor. Bring home the most succulent fruits, perkiest vegetables, freshest fish and meat from the market, then select a recipe from this book, put on your apron and begin cooking.

Convenience is a key consideration. You will save time and money because you can pick up the ingredients in a single stop at the supermarket. The phrase "available at specialty shops" does not appear in these pages.

Wine is a flavor component of many recipes, from everyday meals to company dishes. Wine is essential for good taste in these recipes, not just something added to boost ordinary fare into the "gourmet" realm.

As you cook your way through the book, wine will begin taking its place in your kitchen alongside favorite herbs and spices. Soon, you'll find yourself adding a dash, a tablespoon, a cup to other recipes as you create your own dishes. Instead of asking, "How can I cook with wine?" you'll say with confidence, "Sure I'm cooking with wine. What'll it be today?"

There's More Than Recipes

Besides the delicious and healthy recipes, the book recommends wines to complement your entrées. It also suggests other recipes, many of them from these very pages, to help you plan a complete meal.

The Flavor Formula, in the chapter "Be A Matchmaker" shows how to happily match food and wine in a perfect marriage.

The chapters "Serving Wines" and "A Dozen Questions (And Answers) About Cooking With Wine" answer frequently asked questions and provide guidance in entertaining and cooking.

Whether you're a newcomer to the kitchen or an expert at the cutting board, you'll find the recipes in this book recapture one of life's great pleasures—good food, well prepared, shared with those you love.

—Arlene Mueller

Arlene Mueller

Arlene Mueller, a food and wine writer, contributes articles to newspapers and magazines and edits "Meet Delicato," a bi-monthly newsletter of recipes and wine news. Her dessert cookbook, *Pies & Cakes,* has sold over 100,000 copies. Her culinary style combines the wholesome simplicity of home cooking with novel touches from European and California cuisine. She believes even the simplest meal is an opportunity for celebrating life and love.

About Wine

A Dozen Questions About Cooking With Wine

Q: What wine should I use for cooking?
A. Most wines can be used for cooking, but if you're new to cooking with wine, start with three basic wines: Chenin blanc, Zinfandel, and a dry or medium-dry California sherry.

Q: Will recipes taste better if I use a premium or expensive wine?
A: A good wine will give the same fine flavor to a dish as a premium wine, so save the premium wine to serve with the meal. Only use wines in cooking that you would enjoy drinking.

Q: What is "cooking sherry"?
A: "Cooking sherry" usually has salt or chemicals added to make it unpalatable as a sipping wine (and keep the kitchen help sober). Sold in small bottles, it is generally more expensive than regular sherry. We do not recommend using anything labeled "cooking wine".

Q: Does marinating with wine make a difference?
A: Yes. A wine marinade accents flavors and helps tenderize meat. It is particularly good for accentuating individual fruit flavors and maintaining natural fruit colors. You can often strain and reserve a marinade as an addition to the cooking pot or final sauce.

Q: At what point in the recipe should I add wine?
A: For a mellow flavor, add wine at the start of the cooking process.
  • To achieve a more pronounced wine flavor, reduce the wine by heating it in an uncovered pan. (One cup of wine will reduce to 1/2 cup in 5 minutes.) Stir the reduced wine into the food at the very end of cooking and remove from heat to stop the cooking process.
  • To give an intense flavor to soups, gravies or sauces, add wine as you remove the food from the heat, when the cooking process is complete.
  • Serve a small glass of sherry alongside soups and invite your guests to stir in as much as they wish.
  • Stir wine into pan drippings for a quick sauce or gravy.
  • Wine should be added before milk, cream, eggs or butter to avoid curdling or separation.
  • Add heated wine (hot, but not boiling) to meat dishes as a tenderizer.
  • Brown the meat before adding wine.

Mama and Papa's wedding picture, 1921.

Q: *Will wine in food make me tipsy?*
A: No. The alcohol in wine begins to evaporate at 172° F—well short of the 212° F boiling point of water. Even people who avoid drinking wine for religious or personal reason can cook with wine.

Q: *Will I gain weight if I cook with wine?*
A: Not from the wine. As the alcohol disappears, so do most of the calories. A dry dinner wine will lose 85 percent of its original calories as the alcohol evaporates. The remaining 15 percent of the calories are from non-alcohol substances in the wine.

Q: *Can I use leftover wine for cooking?*
A: Yes. To save leftover wine for cooking, pour into smaller bottles, cork tightly and store in the refrigerator. However, never use spoiled or "turned" wine.

Q: *Should all cooking wines be kept in the refrigerator after they are opened?*
A: Yes, with the exception of sherry. Because of its higher alcohol content (about 20 percent), a partly filled bottle of sherry will keep several months in the cupboard after opening. However, if your kitchen gets hot (in the summer, for example), store the sherry in the refrigerator.

   If you keep wine on hand *just for cooking,* float a thin film of cooking oil on the surface to seal off the wine from the air.

Q. *Can I add wine to any recipe?*
A. Some wine enthusiasts maintain that all foods improve with the addition of wine. Experiment with a familiar recipe to see how wine changes flavors. You can then decide how much and when to incorporate wine into your recipes.

Q. *How much wine should I add?*
A. That depends upon the flavor intensity of the wine and the foods you are cooking. Proceed slowly in trying new combinations. Wine needs time to impart its flavor. If you're not sure whether to add more wine, let the dish cook at least ten minutes before tasting again.

   You wouldn't alter the amount of sugar, flour, baking soda or onions in a recipe without tasting, so don't add wine to a recipe without careful consideration. Adding more wine than the recipe calls for won't make it better.

   Wine does not automatically turn an ordinary dish into a gourmet dish. Use it with discretion.

Suggested amounts:
Soups—2 tablespoons per cup
Sauces—1 tablespoon per cup
Gravies—2 tablespoons per cup
Stews and Meats—1/4 cup per pound
Poaching liquid for fish—1/2 cup per quart

THE EARLY YEARS

People came to the house all the time to visit with Dad. The house would be filled with the Italian language, for most of the folks' friends were immigrants, too, and although Dad learned English, Mom never did.

Mom boiled strong coffee—strained it, then added lots of cream and sugar—and Dad got out a jug of his red wine.

After pouring everyone a small tumbler, just like the ones our relatives still use in Sicily, he set the jug on the floor by his chair. He was in charge of the wine, and never failed to notice when a glass needed refilling.

Dad loved food and wine. "Let's eat," he'd say with a hearty laugh, "for that's all we have in this world."

As the visitors sat around the big table laughing and talking, Dad would lean back and light up a black Toscannelli cigar.

When the guests prepared to leave, he filled boxes with vegetables and fruits from his garden for them to take along. "This doesn't cost anything," he'd say. "We've never been short of food."

When following a recipe, include wine in the total liquid ingredients, not as an extra amount. If you add wine, deduct a like amount of other liquid from the recipe.

Sherry has a more intense flavor than red or white wine, so it should be used in smaller amounts. For example, 2 tablespoons of sherry has the same flavor intensity as 1/2 cup of red or white wine.

Q. Does wine require special cookware?
A. No. Wine has no effect on cookware. However, it is best to marinate in glass, porcelain, enamel or stainless containers rather than in aluminum. Marinating in aluminum cookware might affect the taste of the food.

Be A Matchmaker

Consider two things when "marrying" wine to food. First, match your food with a wine that *complements* it so there will be no struggle between the two. The old adage, "Opposites attract," does not apply here. You don't want a robust Petite Sirah saying to the delicately flavored pork roast, "I'm the strongest!" Instead, the pork roast should join with a milder red, such as a fruity Zinfandel, so they can sing together: "We make a great pair."

Second, match the wine with the food so that *neither loses its unique flavor.* Cabernet Sauvignon, a full-bodied red wine, is smooth, with no discernable acidity when drunk alone or with tart foods. But pair the Cabernet to a ham glazed with candied fruit sauce, and the same wine will taste unpleasantly acidic because of the contrast. Like a good marriage, the paring is most successful when both members retain their own characteristics, yet contribute to the total combination.

Follow the Flavor Formula: Food Flavor Intensity + Wine Flavor Intensity = Balance.

Papa, second from right.

Choosing the right wine for the right meal is more than following the simple rule, "Red wine with red meat, white wine with white meat, and rosé wines with either."

The secret of successful matchmaking is to pair flavor intensities: Delicate food with a Delicate wine, Moderate food with a Moderate wine, and Abundant food with an Abundant wine.

First identify the food flavor intensity. Venison, mackerel, salami, garlic, broccoli and papaya, for example, have Abundant flavor intensities. No sauce or accompanying dish can tone down these assertive flavors. These foods call for an Abundant wine.

The flavor intensity of some foods is determined by the spices, herbs, sauces, and method of preparation. Beef, for example, has a distinct flavor but can be classified Moderate or Abundant, depending on how it is prepared. If the beef is grilled with a simple wine sauce it would be a Moderate-flavor food. However, if the sauce included Worcestershire, capers, or horseradish, the flavor would become Abundant and call for a bigger, Abundant wine.

Consider the egg, which in today's supermarket world is often bland. Poach one and serve it simply on toast with light sprinklings of salt and pepper and you have a Delicate-flavor dish.

Include Hollandaise Sauce and ham for Eggs Benedict and you've produced a Moderate-flavor dish.

Scramble an egg with onions and spicy sausage and you have an Abundant-flavor food.

Visualize three simple pizza crusts: top one with Mozzarella cheese and fresh mushrooms. On the second crust, place the same amount of cheese and mushrooms but add onions and green peppers. The third crust gets all the ingredients plus anchovies and pepperoni. Each pizza represents a flavor intensity level and requires a different wine.

Matching wine and food intensities, you might make these combinations:

Delicate pizza: Mozzarella and mushrooms = White Zinfandel
Moderate pizza: Add on onions and green peppers = Burgundy
Abundant pizza: Add on anchovies and pepperoni = Zinfandel

Next, match a wine with your recipe, following the Flavor Formula so the food and wine flavors will complement each other while maintaining the unique characteristics of both.

After you've identified the flavor intensity, match a wine with your recipe, following the Flavor Formula (Food Flavor Intensity + Wine Flavor Intensity = Balance) so the food and wine flavors will complement each other while maintaining the unique characteristics of both.

Here is a list of common California wines identified by flavor intensity:

WINES ON A PICNIC

What Kind of Wine?

Although you should drink what you like any time of year, most people prefer light-bodied wines during the summer months. Try these favorite *Delicato* picnic wines: *Green Hungarian* (with fruits and seafood salads), *French Colombard* (with chicken dishes), *White Zinfandel* (with cheeses and fruits), *Zinfandel* (with barbecued meats).

Delicato white wines make excellent warm-weather cocktails. Just pour wine over ice and add a twist of lemon. Like red wines? You can turn any red into a wine cooler by adding ice and soda water.

Family portrait, circa 1939.

FLAVOR INTENSITY OF POPULAR CALIFORNIA WINES

DELICATE	MODERATE	ABUNDANT
Whites		
Chablis	Chardonnay	Chardonnay
Chenin blanc	Green Hungarian	Green Hungarian
Rhine	Rhine	
Champagne	Champagne	
	Sauvignon blanc	Sauvignon blanc
	Fumé blanc	
	Gewürztraminer	Gewürztraminer
	Johannisberg Reisling	
	French Colombard	
*Blush Wines**		
	White Cabernet	
	White Zinfandel	
Rosés		
Rosé of Cabernet	Rosé of Cabernet	
Vin Rosé	Vin Rosé	
Reds		
Gamay Beaujolais	Gamay Beaujolais	
	Burgundy	Burgundy
	Zinfandel	
	Pinot noir	
		Petite Sirah
		Barberone
		Merlot
		Cabernet Sauvignon

*Blush wines, relatively new on the wine scene, are lighter than rosés and usually offer more pizazz than chablis or Chenin blanc. These salmon-colored wines (sometimes tending toward copper tones), are fresh and fruity. They should be drunk young.

Some wines, like Zinfandel, appear in more than one category because winemaking styles, micro-climates and blending practices differ. A Zinfandel from one winery may be light and fruity (Moderate), while a Zinfandel from another winery is hearty and assertive (Abundant). As you become acquainted with individual wine varieties and wineries, you will be able to predict the flavor intensity of a particular wine.

In short, a rose is a rose, but a rosé may not always taste the same.

A Perfectly Matched Chicken.

A perfect match takes into account not only the meat, fish or poultry, but also the accompanying dishes, the herbs, spices, sauces and the method of preparation.

Chicken is traditionally paired with white wine. Yet, when using the Flavor Formula (e.g. Delicate + Delicate = Balance), you could come up with all these tasty combinations:

DELICATE-FLAVOR FOOD WITH DELICATE-FLAVOR WINE:

Chicken With Okra (page 81). Lightly sautéed chicken pieces are touched lightly with garlic and onion and combined with the fresh green flavor of okra. Serve with rice and steamed carrots.
Wine: White Cabernet.

or

Chicken In Port (page 78). Creamy chicken pieces with the sweetness of onions and raisins. Serve with brown rice and chopped spinach dusted with nutmeg.
Wine: Green Hungarian or Rosé of Cabernet.

MODERATE-FLAVOR FOOD WITH MODERATE-FLAVOR WINE:

Chicken With Nutmeg (page 79). Onion sweetness combined with cilantro, nutmeg and sherry demand this chicken match up with a smooth and lightly assertive red wine.
Wine: California burgundy.

or

Roast Chicken With Sesame Sauce (page 77). Serve this crisp bird with a potato soufflé and spinach-bacon salad.
Wine: Sauvignon blanc or the same Chenin blanc you use in the sauce.

ABUNDANT-FLAVOR FOOD WITH ABUNDANT-FLAVOR WINE:

Chicken On The Hot Side (page 85). Although simmered and baked in white wine, this chicken lights up with pepper and Tabasco. Serve over fettuccine, with crisp salad greens.
Wine: A hearty Zinfandel or Cabernet Sauvignon.

or

Mustard Chicken (page 76). Prepared with Chenin blanc, country-style Dijon mustard and sour cream. Serve with mounds of white rice, sautéed carrots and zucchini.
Wine: Petite Sirah.

Make Friends With Your Taste Memory

Taste memory, which is your personal ability to remember the taste of a particular dish, plays an important role in choosing a wine.

Each of us craves certain dishes on our birthday, holidays or rainy days. There are foods, too, we need when we're depressed, lonesome or very happy.

Think of your special foods. Close your eyes and try to "taste" one of them. Enjoy an imaginary "bite." Chew a while and then take a second "bite." Focus on the dominant flavor. Is it salty, sweet, nutty, gamey? Or is an herb, perhaps tarragon, foremost in your taste? Concentrate on that taste. (Selecting the dominant taste of a dish is like identifying the dominant hue in a piece of plaid cloth—as you squint at it, one color will predominate.) When you've identified the dominant taste, memorize it.

Next, reach for an imaginary glass of wine to accompany your taste. Choose whatever wine your taste memory suggests, perhaps a chilled, oak-aged Chardonnay, a fruity Zinfandel or a lightly sweet Green Hungarian.

Practice memorizing the tastes of wine and foods at meals. Eventually you'll be able to read a recipe and "taste" a wine to match it.

Keep notes on food and wine tastes in your recipe file, in the margins of your cookbooks, or in a separate notebook just for this purpose. Jot down reactions to food and wine combinations you've created. Make suggestions to yourself for other wines that would be companionable.

Soon food and wine will go together easily, and you'll avoid those last-minute decisions and frantic late-afternoon wine purchases. Eventually, you may want to start your own cellar so you can have your favorite wines on hand.

A Final Word

There are no firm and fast rules for matching wine and food, only guidelines and suggestions. Your personal taste in both food and drink must determine your final choice.

Vincent Indelicato with aunt who lives in Sicily.

Serving Wine

Today, most entertaining is dictated not by etiquette books but by individual tastes. The way you serve wine should reflect your own style of hospitality. Here are some simple suggestions that will make your wine service more attractive while preserving a touch of tradition.

Which Wines?

First decide on a menu, then choose the wine. If you have your own cellar, get the wines out in the morning and place them upright. If you are purchasing wines, buy them the day before serving, since wines don't like movement or temperature changes before they're opened.

How Much Wine?

The standard wine bottle is 750 ml, one "fifth" of a gallon, or 25 ounces. This will provide four servings, using the eight or nine-ounce all-purpose glass.

Champagne portions are generally smaller, so you can serve six guests from each 750 ml bottle.

For a dinner preceded by drinks or aperitifs, plan on one-fourth bottle per guest. If dinner is to be leisurely, with several courses, allow one-half bottle per person. If you are serving several wines, determine quantity in the same way, allowing one-fourth bottle per guest for each course. Amounts vary, of course, according to the length of the dinner and the desire of the diner.

What Temperature?

The "room temperature" often recommended for red dinner wines is actually closer to cellar temperature (65°F). If your reds are coming from a cooler storage area, bring them out a few hours before serving and let them warm up to 65°F. If your reds are too warm, chill them briefly in the refrigerator. Watch the temperature, however: chilling red wines below 65°F brings out the tannin and results in a harsher taste.

White dinner wines should be chilled to 55°F and brought directly from the refrigerator to the table or to an ice bucket. Whites lose their bouquet, and consequently their best taste, if they get too cold.

Rosés are best served slightly more chilled at 45°F.

Champagne and sparkling wines must be served cold, cold, cold—35°F.

Ideal Serving Temperatures
Red wine   65°F
White Wine   55°F
Rosé Wine   45°F
Champagne   35-45°F

These temperatures are ideals. You can check the temperature in your refrigerator with an outdoor thermometer. Place it on top, middle and bottom shelves to see which area is best.

How To Chill?

Champagnes and white wines can be quickly chilled in an ice bucket filled equally with ice and water. Total immersion and rotation insure quick chilling.

As a last resort for a fast chill if no ice bucket is available, put the bottles in the freezer compartment of your refrigerator for a half hour. Set your timer so you don't forget them.

Place an ice bucket near the table to keep white and rosé wines and champagne cold throughout the meal. Or, for a less formal occasion, use a terra cotta wine cooler to keep wines cool at the table without ice.

What Order To Serve Wines?

If you are serving several wines with your meal, you may want to follow the traditional rule: white before red, young before old, light before robust, and dry before sweet.

WINES ON A PICNIC

What Temperature?

In summer, serve white wines icy cold. Here's how to keep wine chilled on a picnic:

1) Chill the wine bottle in your freezer for 20 minutes before leaving home, then place it in your cooler with ice.
2) Soak several pages of newspaper in water until limp. Wrap the bottle securely and place it in your freezer until the paper is "crisp." Wrap in a towel and place in your picnic basket. The wine will stay chilled for hours.
3) Place chilled wine bottle in insulated containers especially designed for wine travel.
4) Or, go natural—tie a rope around your bottle and let it bob in the cold stream or lake.

To Serve...

If your picnic is an elegant affair, wrap wine glasses in napkins. If you're going casual, use flat-bottomed, clear plastic glasses or small jelly glasses. Pour small portions and offer refills to keep the wine chilled.

In this fashion you advance from delicately flavored foods and wines to more complex, abundantly flavored ones. The dessert wines— sweet sherries, ports or fruit wines—are sweeter and heavier and go well at the meal's conclusion. Remember, these are only general guides. Your taste may suggest other ways of serving.

What Kind Of Glasses And Where Do They Go?

An all-purpose, eight to nine-ounce glass will do for all types of wine, including sherry and champagne. The tulip shape, narrower at the bottom and top, captures the wine's appealing aroma (sense of smell accounts for ninety percent of our taste sensation).

If you want to expand your glassware collection, add tall champagne flutes. This shape of glass keeps the wine bubbling happily.

Another useful glass to have is the balloon bowl glass, also called the big Burgundy glass. This large, open bowl gives ample room for robust reds to stretch comfortably. (Don't get carried away by the size when you pour: fill only one-third full, leaving space to swish the wine and encourage the aroma.)

The hock or Rhine glass, a small bowl atop a long stem, is traditional for Rieslings and Gewürztraminers.

Clear glass is best since it reveals the natural color of the wine. Stemmed glasses keep hands from warming the wine and the bowl clear of finger prints.

If you have separate wine glasses for each wine, line them up to the right of the water goblet. Pour the first wine into the glass farthest to the right. Remove it from the table when you pour the next wine. Fill glasses half-full for dinner wines and one-third full for sherries and champagne.

If you're serving more than one wine in the same glass, it is prudent to remove and rinse it out between each wine.

At the Table

If you open your wine at the table, cut neatly below the first ridge of the bottle neck through the "capsule" (the lead or plastic cover over the cork) with a knife, wipe the mouth of the bottle with a clean napkin, then uncork the bottle. Unless you have some practice with other types of openers, choose a "wing-type" (one with arms that go up and down)—it will make the job easier. Pour a bit into your glass first, taste it for flavor and temperature, then fill your guests' glasses no more than half full, allowing space to swirl the wine.

If you're serving from a decanter, there's no need to pour the first glassful. Simply urge your guests to help themselves, and refill the decanter as needed.

Decanting Your Wines

It is said that a good wine deserves decanting, and an ordinary wine requires it. Decanting is done for two reasons: to improve the appearance of a wine, and to bring out taste, aroma and bouquet.

Older red wines (over ten years old) are often decanted to remove sediment, the microscopic particles of grapes that gradually settle to the bottom during long storage. Young wines and white wines seldom have noticeable sediment, but their appearance can be enhanced by serving them in an attractive decanter. Jug wines are usually decanted both for the sake of appearance and to make pouring easier.

Storing Leftover Wine

If you have dinner wine left, cork the bottle tightly and drink it the next day. For storage up to a week, decant to a smaller bottle to eliminate the air space above the wine. Store in the refrigerator, where it will keep for several days to a week. Best of all, finish the wine when you open it.

Because of the higher alcoholic content, dessert wines will keep on the shelf or in the refrigerator for a month or two.

Don't subject leftover wines to temperature changes. Choose one place and keep them there.

Barbecuing With Wine

Wine Marinades

What Do Marinades Do?

Marinating is a simple way to enhance the natural flavor of meat, fish, or poultry with wine, spices, and herbs. Because of the natural acidity in wine, wine marinades also help tenderize food. Extending marinating time will not totally tenderize meat for the tough connective tissue—collagen—can only be dissolved by heat.

Does Marinating Take Special Skill?

No. Most marinades are quite simple. Just place your meat, poultry, or fish in a glass or porcelain bowl. Pour enough wine over the meat to barely cover it. Add your choice of herbs and spices, cover the bowl, and let the marinade do the rest. All you have to do is turn the food occasionally with a wooden spoon. When the time is up, remove the food from the marinade, pat it dry with paper towels, and grill, bake, or sauté.

Which Wines Work Best?

Most dinner wines may be used for marinating. California burgundy, Zinfandel, and Chablis blanc are good choices. Wine left over from a recent meal makes an excellent marinade. Keep in mind that red wines will darken foods.

SUMMERTIME SANGRIA

1 bottle California Zinfandel or
California burgundy 750 ml
2 ounces brandy (optional)
1/4 cup sugar
1 lime, thinly sliced
1 lemon, thinly sliced
1 orange, thinly sliced
1/2 cup orange juice
1 cup club soda, chilled
Ice cubes

Combine wine, brandy, sugar, fruit, and juice in large pitcher. Refrigerate for 1 hour. Remove fruit to avoid bitterness. Add club soda at serving time and pour over ice cubes. Garnish with fruit from beverage or with fresh seasonal fruit such as peaches, plums or strawberries. Makes 8 generous servings.

Four or five hours is enough time for an average portion of meat or poultry (1 to 6 servings). Two hours is long enough for most fish. Food left in the marinade for longer periods does not become more tender. However, even a half hour of marinating will improve flavor. Meats may marinate at room temperature up to 2 hours; beyond that they should be refrigerated. Always refrigerate fish and poultry.

Should Marinades Be Saved?
Yes. Strain, refrigerate, and use within two weeks. Strained marinades may also be thickened with egg yolk, arrowroot, or cornstarch, creating a sauce. Oils and butters may also be added to marinades, creating a baste for cooking.

A BASIC MARINADE:

This recipe—using red or white wine—has the basic ingredients of a tasty marinade. Try it—and then adjust it with your favorite herbs and spices.

1 carrot, thinly sliced
1 large onion, sliced
2 cloves garlic, crushed
Sprig parsley
2 stalks celery, sliced (optional)
6-8 peppercorns
1 bay leaf
1 whole clove
Pinch thyme
2-1/2 cups California burgundy*.

Mix all ingredients together in a jar. Pour over meat, poultry, or fish to barely cover. *When marinating poultry, veal, pork and some fish, substitute Chablis blanc and use marjoram in place of thyme.

VARIATIONS:

Simple Barbecue for Meat and Poultry

8 ounces tomato sauce
1/2 cup California burgundy
1 teaspoon dry mustard

Marinate 1-4 hours in refrigerator. Bake or grill.

DISCOVER ANCIENT MESQUITE

Grilling over mesquite charcoal is a tasty alternative to pan frying.

Mesquite wood, from the Sonora desert of Mexico, has been used since ancient times for preparing meats. Settlers in the area first learned how to use it from the Indians living there.

Now, as modern cooks rediscover this venerable fuel, it has become available in food specialty shops and even in some supermarkets. Mesquite burns with a hotter flame than regular charcoal, so watch the trout carefully to avoid overcooking. Because it contains no filler, as regular charcoal often does, mesquite imparts a delicious, natural wood smoke flavor that combines nicely with the delicate marinade.

Beef Shortribs

1/2 cup peanut or sesame oil
1/4 cup soy sauce
1/2 cup California dry sherry
Minced garlic to taste

Marinate 2-5 hours in refrigerator. Grill.

More Beef Shortribs

1/4 cup soy sauce
1/4 cup Chablis blanc
1 clove garlic
2 tablespoons sesame seeds
2 green onions, thinly sliced

Marinate 4-5 hours in refrigerator. Grill or broil.

Poultry, Shellfish, Veal, Beef

1/2 cup soy sauce
1/2 cup California dry sherry
2 tablespoons vegetable oil
1 chopped garlic clove
1/2 teaspoon freshly grated ginger

Marinate 2 hours at room temperature. Grill or broil.

Chicken

1/3 cup olive oil
1/3 cup fresh lemon juice
1 minced garlic clove
1 teaspoon thyme
5 chopped green onions
1 cup Chablis blanc
1/2 teaspoon salt
5-8 peppercorns
1 strip lemon peel

Marinate 2 hours at room temperature. Bake or grill.

Chicken

1/3 cup Chablis blanc
1/3 cup pineapple juice
1/4 cup lemon juice
2 tablespoons soy sauce
1 clove garlic

Marinate 2 hours at room temperature. Bake.

In the sixties we introduced our "Tingle," a popular aperitif wine and forerunner of the wine cooler. This twenty-percent lemon-flavored white wine became an instant success. We quit making it in the last decade, but are bringing it back because our customers have continued to ask for it.

Lamb Kebabs

1/3 cup melted butter
3 tablespoons Chablis blanc
1/4 teaspoon tumeric
1/8 teaspoon ground ginger
1/4 teaspoon curry powder

Marinate 2 hours at room temperature. Skewer with green peppers and pineapple chunks. Grill or broil.

Lamb Chops

1/3 cup melted butter
2 tablespoons California port
2 tablespoons orange juice
1/8 teaspoon nutmeg
1/4 teaspoon ground cinnamon
1 clove garlic
2 bay leaves
Marinate 2 hours at room temperature. Grill or broil.

Salmon Steaks

1/2 cup Chablis blanc
1/3 cup vegetable oil
2 teaspoons parsley
1/2 teaspoon tarragon
2 teaspoons salt
1/4 teaspoon dill seeds

Marinate 1-1/2 hours in refrigerator. Grill or broil. Baste with melted butter or remaining strained marinade.

STRAWBERRY SANGRIA

1 cup thinly sliced strawberries
1/2 cup sugar
1 whole lemon, thinly sliced
1 bottle Delicato Zinfandel (750 ml)
2 cups club soda

In large bowl combine strawberries, sugar and lemon slices. Stir mixture, bruising the fruit lightly. Pour in wine, cover and chill at least 1 hour. Remove lemon slices.

In punch bowl or large pitcher, blend wine mixture with club soda. Add ice to glasses. Ladle or pour wine into glasses. Serves 6.

Appetizers

Antipasto Tray

Let your guests linger over the antipasto course long enough for everyone to sample all the appetizing delicacies and become familiar with the hearty red you've chosen.

Suggested Foods:

Green onions
Small sardines in oil
Black and green olives
Tuna, unmolded from can on lettuce leaves
Mortadella slices, rolled and fastened with toothpicks
Salami sliced very thin
Caponata (page 30)
Marinated mushrooms
Parsley

Cover a large platter with lettuce leaves. Place tuna in center, arranging other foods around it in a sunburst design, or arrange items in a striped effect across the plate. Tuck in parsley sprigs for garnish.

Vary the selection with favorite or seasonal foods. This piquant first course will prepare appetites for the pasta course to follow.

Mama and Papa with youngest son.

Artichoke Bites

1 can artichoke hearts packed in water, drained (14 ounces)
1/3 cup Sauvignon blanc
1/4 cup finely grated Parmesan cheese
1/2 cup unseasoned bread crumbs
1/4 cup olive oil

Preheat oven to 400°. If using whole artichoke hearts, quarter or halve them into bite-size pieces. Soak in wine while preparing crumbs and cheese. Mix cheese and crumbs together in a dish. Place oil in a separate shallow dish. Lightly oil cookie sheet with vegetable oil or butter.

Remove pieces one at a time from wine. Shake gently, then dip into oil and roll lightly in crumb-cheese mixture. Place on cookie sheet about 1/2 inch apart.

Bake for 15 minutes or until lightly brown. Serve immediately with crisp whole wheat crackers. Makes about 32 quarter hearts.

Wine Suggestion: California Sauvignon blanc or Chardonnay.

Biscotti

6 cups flour, sifted
1-1/2 cups sugar
1-1/2 teaspoons salt
6 teaspoons baking powder
1/4 teaspoon black pepper
12 tablespoons shortening or 1-1/2 cubes margarine
6 eggs, beaten
1/4 cup California brandy
1 egg yolk
2 tablespoons milk

Mix flour with sugar, salt, baking powder, and pepper. Cut in shortening. Place eggs and brandy in center of mixture. Mix thoroughly. Tear off enough dough to create a 1/2 x 6-inch "rope." Create a "doughnut" by joining ends. Make 24 doughnuts.

Place on greased baking sheet. Mix egg yolk with 2 tablespoons milk and brush top with egg wash. Bake 20 to 30 minutes at 350° until golden. Makes 2 dozen biscuits.

Wine Suggestion: Delicato Chenin Blanc.

BISCOTTI

"I was not only the oldest child, but the only girl as well. I learned to make Italian dishes such as *biscotti* by cooking alongside Mom every day.

"Dad came from Campobello, Sicily while Mom and her sisters grew up in Moliterno, about thirty miles from Naples. When they married in this country, our kitchen became an Italian melting pot. Mom cooked some dishes her mother had taught her and some Sicilian recipes to please Dad. Pasta was the common denominator, of course.

"We always ate the *biscotti* with coffee or wine. I love them with morning coffee, the second day, when they're a bit dried out."
—Frances Indelicato Sciabica

Garlic Galore

Cooked garlic loses its punch, mellowing into a nutty sweetness. Keep the leftover garlic refrigerated in a covered jar. Add a clove or two to spaghetti sauce or vegetables.

6 tablespoons olive oil
6 tablespoons unsalted butter
6 heads garlic, unpeeled
6 tablespoons California dry white wine
French bread slices, toasted

Heat oil and butter in a pan large enough to allow garlic heads to touch comfortably on one layer. Sauté garlic heads for several minutes, turning often until they are coated with butter and oil and tinged light brown.

Add wine and bring to a boil. Lower heat and simmer covered over very low heat for several hours.

To serve, place hot garlic with sauce in a communal bowl and urge your guests to help themselves. Pop softened garlic from skins and mash with a fork. Spread on toasted French bread. Enjoy with a bold red wine and goat cheeses.

Wine Suggestion: California Petite Sirah or robust Zinfandel.

Brie Pinwheel

Small round of Brie
Golden raisins
Dill weed
Slivered almonds

Remove the white skin on Brie with a knife. Score the surface into 3 parts, pie-fashion. Arrange raisins on one section, dill on another, and almonds on the third. Refrigerate until half hour before serving. Serve with unsalted crackers. Increase size of round for more guests, adding other toppings of your choice.

Wine Suggestion: California Chardonnay.

Caponata

Mama's family.

Wonderful, unusual flavors with a nice celery crunch. Chocolate mellows the mixture, but no one will guess it's there.

1 large eggplant cut into 1-inch cubes (about 3 cups)
Salt
1 tablespoon olive oil
3 cups celery, cut into 1/4-inch slices
1 tablespoon sugar
1-1/2 teaspoons capers
2 tablespoons chopped black olives
2 tablespoons wine vinegar
1-1/2 tablespoons grated, unsweetened chocolate
Salt and pepper

Peel eggplant and cut into 1-inch cubes. Sprinkle with salt and place on a plate. Put another plate over eggplant and weight down to encourage weeping. Leave for 1 hour. Rinse eggplant pieces to remove salt, and pat dry. Heat olive oil in skillet and fry eggplant until brown and soft. Remove and reserve.
    Add sliced celery to same pan and fry until soft. Stir in eggplant, mixing well. Add sugar, capers, olives, vinegar and chocolate. Season with salt and pepper to taste. Mix well and chill. Serve as a vegetable or condiment with cold meats or chicken. Also good on thin slices of French bread or on unsalted crackers.

Wine Suggestion: Robust Zinfandel.

Carpaccio

An elegant first course that goes together in minutes.

1/2 pound lean, boneless, uncooked filet mignon, *very thinly sliced**
4 anchovies, drained and minced
1/4 cup olive oil
2 tablespoons lemon juice
2 tablespoons capers
4 tablespoons minced onion
6 black olives
4 lemon wedges
Minced parsley for garnish
French bread, baguette-size loaf, thinly sliced
Unsalted butter
Salt and pepper to taste
4 lemon wedges

Lightly overlap meat slices on one part of four salad plates. Place minced anchovies on top. Combine olive oil and lemon juice and drizzle over meat. Make small mounds of capers and onions on empty side of plate. Garnish with black olives, lemon wedge and parsley.

Place beef on buttered bread. Add desired condiments and a squeeze of lemon. Pass the grinder, for a light dusting of fresh pepper. Makes 4 servings.

Wine Suggestion: Serve with a robust California red wine such as a Petite Sirah or Cabernet Sauvignon.

**Your butcher can slice the thinnest beef. If you're slicing it, partially freeze the meat first.*

We lived a simple life. Because we had little money, our daily meals were pretty much the same. We ate lots of bread. Every day at six o'clock in the morning, Muzio's bakery truck from Stockton delivered ten loaves of crusty bread.

For many years, eleven of us, six Indelicatos and five Luppinos, lived in the small frame house where there is now a parking lot.

"Uncle," as we called Sebastiano Luppino, was the breakfast cook and he usually made us kids bacon and eggs. Sometimes, though, he'd fix eggs with home-cured black olives. Every day he'd call, "Breakfast ready. First call," like the porters on the trains he often rode to the East Coast to sell grapes.

If no one appeared, he'd say "Breakfast ready. Last call." When we finally stumbled sleepily into the kitchen the eggs were hard and cold, but they still tasted good to us.

Vince in first grade, Tony in fifth grade, circa 1939.

Cozzula

"*Cozzula* was a special dish that we had at Easter and was from Mom's region of Italy. When we were small, Mom got the cheese from our neighbors, and today I still make an effort to find fresh bulk Ricotta. It makes a difference."
—Frances Indelicato Sciabica

2 pounds Ricotta cheese (preferably fresh bulk)
1/4 cup sugar
3 tablespoons chopped parsley
1/2 teaspoon salt
1 egg yolk
4 hard-cooked eggs, thinly sliced
1 tablespoon cinnamon
4 tablespoons sugar
1 egg yolk, beaten
Pastry dough

PASTRY DOUGH:

5 cups flour
1/2 cup sugar
1/2 teaspoon salt
1 package dry yeast
1 tablespoon shortening
2 cups warm water—120° to 130°

Blend Ricotta, sugar, parsley, salt and egg yolk. Set aside.

Prepare pastry dough: Mix flour, sugar, salt and dry yeast. Cut in shortening. Add warm water and blend well. Shape into balls, one slightly larger, and set aside in greased bowls, covered with a damp cloth, in a draft-free area until dough doubles in size.

Lightly flour rolling pin and surface. Roll larger dough ball into 1/2-inch thick rectangle. Lay in buttered 9 x 13-inch pan, bringing dough up sides of pan with 1/2-inch overlap.

Spread Ricotta mixture on crust. Add sliced eggs on top. Mix cinnamon and sugar and sprinkle over eggs.

Roll out remaining dough. Lay on top of cheese mixture and eggs, fluting it firmly with bottom crust. Brush top with beaten egg yolk. Pierce top crust with fork. Bake 40 to 50 minutes at 350°. Cool at room temperature. Refrigerate until serving time. Makes 24 squares.

Wine Suggestion: Delicato Green Hungarian.

Chicken Wings

Pick these up with your fingers and enjoy the zippy succulence.

10 to 12 plump chicken wings
1/4 cup Delicato Cream Sherry
1/4 cup light soy sauce (it's less salty than regular soy sauce)
4 star anise*
2 thin slices fresh ginger root

Rinse and dry chicken wings, then place in single layer under broiler. Broil until crisp, turning at least once. Wings should be almost completely cooked.

In flat skillet, combine sherry, soy sauce, anise cloves and ginger. Bring to a boil, stirring continually. Reduce heat and add wings. Using tongs, turn wings until well coated and cook until they begin to glisten with soy mixture.

When liquid is almost absorbed, remove wings to heated platter. Serve immediately with plenty of paper napkins. The wings are also a wonderful picnic food, hot or cold. Serves two for dinner or several as an appetizer.

Wine Suggestion: California Green Hungarian.

Available at Oriental markets. They keep for years in a jar.

STAR ANISE

A favorite spice in Chinese cooking, star anise is the fruit of a small evergreen tree. About the size of a quarter, resembling a seven-petaled poinsettia bloom, star anise is dark brown and firm, like wood. Like anise and fennel seed, star anise contains anethole, an oil with licorice flavor. Star anise can be used either whole or ground.

Sherried Walnuts

These crunchy sweet nuts require no cooking. Serve with a sip of sherry or coffee. Sprinkle broken pieces over ice cream and pour on a bit of Delicato Angelica for a quick, luscious dessert.

1-1/2 cups brown sugar
1/4 teaspoon salt
1/4 cup California dry sherry
2 tablespoons light corn syrup
3-1/2 cups walnut *halves*
Granulated sugar

Blend brown sugar, salt, sherry and corn syrup until smooth. Stir in walnuts, mixing until all are well coated. Roll nuts in granulated sugar until lightly frosted. Place on waxed paper to dry.

Oven Spread

1 can chopped black olives (4-1/2 ounces)
1 can chopped Ortega green chilies (4 ounces)
1 can tomato sauce (8 ounces)
3 to 4 garlic cloves, finely minced
2 cups grated Sharp Cheddar cheese
1/4 cup grated Romano cheese

Mix all ingredients. Spread on French bread slices and broil until mixture is bubbly. Cut into hors d'oeuvre pieces. Mary says the mixture freezes well.

Spinach Squares

2 packages chopped frozen spinach (10 ounces each)
6 slices white bread, cut into 1/4-inch cubes
1/2 cup olive oil (don't substitute salad oil)
1 cup milk
6 eggs, beaten
3 to 4 tablespoons dry minced onion
2 teaspoons Italian Seasoning
1 teaspoon salt
1 teaspoon garlic powder
1 teaspoon black pepper
2/3 cup grated Parmesan cheese
Paprika

Preheat oven to 350°. Cook spinach according to package directions and drain well. Combine with white bread cubes. Gradually add all ingredients (except paprika) in order of listing. Spread into greased 8x11-inch pan. Sprinkle generously with paprika. Bake 35 to 45 minutes at 350°. Let cool before cutting into 1-1/2 inch squares.

Wine Suggestion: California Zinfandel.

Hint: Freeze bread slices for easier cutting.

"The family usually gathers at our house for Thanksgiving. We all sit around a large table that takes up almost all the dining room.

"This is the same table where eleven people used to eat every meal: Gaspare and Caterina Indelicato, their four children and the Sam Luppino family which lived with them.

"Gaspare bought the big table so that everyone could be together for meals. Later, when he and Caterina built a new brick home near the winery, they left the oversized piece of furniture in the old frame house. Years later, Tony and I resurrected the big table, refinished it, and brought it into the center of our home.

"While everyone waits for the turkey to be done, I serve appetizers. They're modern, compared to the rest of the traditional meal, but very good with wine. And not filling, so you can do justice to the meal. Italian cooking is not new to me— my maiden name is Celsi, I speak Italian and learned cooking from my mother."

—Mary Indelicato

Soups

Caterina's Minestrone

Sisters, Caterina, Rose, Virginia, 1926.

"It's the *fagioli romani* bean (Roman or cranberry bean) and the curly cabbage that make this soup so good," says Frances, who made it alongside her mother, Caterina Indelicato, for many years.

8 cups boiling water
2 to 3 garlic cloves, minced
1 large onion, chopped fine
1/2 head celery, chopped
2 carrots, chopped
2 cups Swiss chard, coarsely chopped
1 zucchini, peeled and chopped
1/4 cup parsley, minced
4 or more fresh sweet basil leaves, minced
Pinch oregano
2 to 3 fresh tomatoes, skinned and crushed or
    1 can tomatoes with juice (16 ounces)
Salt and pepper to taste
1 pound romani beans, cooked *or* 3 cans red kidney beans with juice
    (16 ounces each)
2 potatoes, cut into quarters, then *one* quarter chopped coarsely
4 cups curly cabbage, coarsely sliced
3 tablespoons olive oil
1 cup uncooked elbow macaroni
Grated Romano cheese

Boil water in a 6 to 8 quart kettle. Add garlic, onion, celery, carrots, Swiss chard, zucchini, parsley, sweet basil, oregano and tomatoes. Cover and simmer for 25 minutes.

Add salt and pepper and beans. Simmer 20 minutes. Last, add curly cabbage and olive oil. Cover and cook 30 minutes, or until cabbage is cooked.

At the same time, but in a separate pot, cook 1 cup elbow macaroni. Combine hot, drained pasta with soup and serve immediately. Pass Romano cheese for those who wish to put some on top of the soup. Serves 6 to 8.

Wine Suggestion: California Zinfandel.

Oyster Chowder

A hearty, creamy soup without a drop of cream.

4 tablespoons butter
3 tablespoons chopped onion
3/4 cup finely cut celery
3 carrots, finely diced
Oyster liquor (reserved from oysters)
1/4 teaspoon thyme
1 cup California dry white wine
2 cups peeled, diced potatoes
1 quart milk, room temperature
1 pint oysters, drained
Salt and pepper to taste
1/3 cup minced parsley for garnish
Paprika

Melt butter in a saucepan and quickly brown onion, celery and carrots. Sauté for 3 minutes. Add oyster liquor, thyme, white wine and bring to a boil. Add potatoes, cover and simmer until tender. Add milk and bring just to the boiling point. Reduce heat, add oysters and cook until their edges curl. Salt and pepper to taste. Pour soup into bowls or a tureen and garnish with chopped parsley and paprika. Makes 4 meal-size servings.

Wine Suggestion: California Chardonnay.

Founder with the two youngest children.

Consommé With Avocado

An elegant beginning for formal dinner parties and so easy to prepare.

2 cans beef broth (14-1/2 ounces each)
6 to 8 tablespoons California dry sherry
1 avocado, peeled and thinly cut into 1/2-inch pieces
2 small green onions, finely minced

Heat broth. Add sherry and simmer for 5 minutes. Divide avocado pieces equally among individual soup bowls. Sprinkle finely minced onions on soup and serve immediately with salted wheat crackers. Serves 4 to 6.

Hint: Also a great take-along for picnics and sports events. Pour heated broth from thermos over diced avocado pieces. Drink the beverage instead of spooning it.

Chilled Apricot Soup

A delicate fruit and a fruity wine pair up for a summertime soup.

1-1/2 cups canned, drained whole or half apricots
   (or same amount pitted fresh apricots)*
3/4 cup Delicato Green Hungarian
1 cup natural unflavored yogurt
1/2 cup whole milk
Nutmeg

Purée apricots with wine in blender or food processor. Transfer to large bowl and whisk in yogurt and milk until smooth. Add milk if necessary to please your taste. Refrigerate covered for at least 1 hour. Ladle soup into small bowls. Grate plenty of fresh nutmeg on surface of each serving. Serves 4 to 6.
   Combine with Oriental Chicken Salad (page 48) and popovers for an exotic lunch.

Wine Suggestion: Delicato Green Hungarian.

Fresh apricots may require a small amount of sugar.

SUMMERTIME SANGRIA

1 bottle California Zinfandel or
   California burgundy (750 ml)
2 ounces brandy (optional)
1/4 cup sugar
1 lime, thinly sliced
1 lemon, thinly sliced
1 orange, thinly sliced
1/2 cup orange juice
1 cup club soda, chilled
Ice cubes

Combine wine, brandy, sugar, fruit, and juice in large pitcher. Refrigerate for 1 hour. Remove fruit to avoid bitterness. Add club soda at serving time and pour over ice cubes. Garnish with fruit from beverage or with fresh seasonal fruit such as peaches, plums or strawberries. Makes 8 generous servings.

Chilled Curried Soup

This exciting soup will stir your blood as well as your appetite!

4 cups homemade chicken broth or 2 cans (14-1/2 ounces each)
4 eggs, well beaten
1/2 cup lemon juice
1/8 teaspoon ground ginger
1/4 teaspoon white pepper
1 teaspoon mild curry powder
2 tablespoons California dry sherry
Finely minced parsley for garnish
Thinly sliced lemon for garnish

Bring chicken broth to a slow boil. Combine beaten eggs with lemon juice. Gradually pour mixture into broth, stirring constantly. Add ginger, pepper and curry powder and remove from heat. Add sherry and chill until icy cold. Just before serving, taste for salt, lemon, and curry and adjust to your taste. Garnish each serving with minced parsley and a lemon slice. Serves 4.

Wine Suggestion: California Chardonnay.

Mushroom Soup

A creamy soup that boasts of fresh mushroom flavor.

1/2 pound fresh mushrooms, finely minced (about 2-1/2 cups)
1/2 cup finely minced onion
1 can chicken broth (14-1/2 ounces), heated
1 teaspoon butter
3 tablespoons butter
3 tablespoons flour
1-3/4 cups milk, heated
Salt and pepper to taste
1/4 cup California dry sherry
Nutmeg

Wipe mushrooms with a damp paper towel. Cut off stems, *reserving 4 caps for garnish*. Mince stems and remaining caps and add with onion to heated broth. Simmer uncovered for 30 minutes.

Slice and sauté remaining caps in 1 teaspoon butter and set aside. Melt 3 tablespoons butter in saucepan. Blend in flour until thick and smooth. Slowly add heated milk, whisking until sauce thickens. Stir thickened sauce into broth, stirring constantly. Taste for seasonings. Simmer for two minutes, continuing to stir. Add sherry and blend well. Ladle hot soup into 4 bowls, add sautéed mushrooms for garnish, grate nutmeg over top and serve immediately. Makes 4 soup servings or 2 hearty lunch portions.

This mushroom soup nicely introduces Easy Pork Chops With Fennel (page 111).

Wine Suggestion: California Sauvignon blanc.

Francy made our lunches for school. As the only Indelicato daughter, she did a lot of work with Mom in the kitchen. Usually we had salami and cheese sandwiches on French bread. Some days, we had plain jelly sandwiches. We were embarrassed by the crusty, thick-sliced bread that labeled us as "immigrant kids." We were surprised, though, when the other kids offered to trade their bologna sandwiches made with thin-sliced white bread for our simpler ones.

When we came home hungry after school, we would barbecue homemade sausages on the coals in the pot-bellied wood stove and fill up on bread. At night we usually had soup, made with whatever was ripe in the garden.

We didn't have much red meat, because that had to be purchased. Instead, we ate lots of chicken and rabbits that we raised on the farm. We always butchered a hog, for sausage and other pork dishes. We were pretty much self-sufficient. There were plenty of vegetables in our garden, so we always ate three good meals a day, even when times were tough.

By the time we boys were ready to attend college, we thought the food at home was pretty ordinary. We were mighty tired of spaghetti and minestrone. But a few weeks of cafeteria food changed all that. On our first visit home, we ate everything in sight.

Children of founders, 1934.

Kale Soup

"I grew up on this hearty, simple Portuguese soup, and now my family loves it, too. My father, Joe Cardoza, who emigrated from the Azores, and my mother, Mary, early in their married life lived on property adjoining the Indelicato land.

"My mother, Mary Cardoza, remembers meeting Gaspare across the fence. She and my father were young and newly married and Gaspare took them under his wing. He'd come over to visit, always bringing whatever he had extra from his garden. At Christmas he brought them a gallon of wine.

"One day, my dad recalls, Gaspare came over to ask if he should buy a cow to supply milk for his family. My dad explained to him about the cost of hay and veterinary bills, even for one cow. Gaspare listened and reasoned it wasn't economical. Instead, he bought milk from my folks who had a dairy farm. That was good for both families. In 1954 Vince and I were married and both families still live near each other and share many family meals."

—Dorothy Indelicato

Caldo Verde

2-1/2 to 3 pounds beef with bones
2-1/2 quarts cold water
Salt and pepper
1 medium onion, chopped
1 tablespoon minced parsley
4 large potatoes, quartered
5 cups kale (or chard), loosely packed
1 tablespoon wine vinegar

Place meat in cold water with salt, pepper, onions and parsley. Simmer for 3 hours. Remove meat and bones. Add potatoes and kale and simmer for 45 minutes. Return meat, add vinegar and serve immediately. Serves 6.

Pumpkin Soup

Autumn pumpkin appears as a holiday dinner first course.

2 cups milk
2 small green onions
2-1/3 cups canned pumpkin
1 cup chicken broth
2 teaspoons butter
Salt and pepper to taste
1 cup finely diced cooked ham
Fresh nutmeg for garnish

In large saucepan, scald milk. Add whole green onions. Stir in pumpkin and blend well. Add broth and heat mixture at low temperature until hot but not boiling. Stir in butter. Season to taste. Add diced ham.

Remove onions and mince very finely for garnish. Ladle soup into serving bowl or individual bowls. Sprinkle onions on top and grate fresh nutmeg in each bowl. Serves 4.

Delicious with Zucchini Bread (page 41).

Wine Suggestion: California Chardonnay or White Cabernet.

Zucchini Bread

Cheryl, Frank and Alice Indelicato's daughter, is studying to be a nurse and likes to cook nutritious foods. Her brother Michael always has a big garden and in this recipe she uses some of the abundant summer zucchini.

1 cup oil
2 cups sugar
3 eggs, beaten
2 cups grated fresh zucchini *or* 1 package frozen sliced zucchini
   (16 ounces), defrosted and run through food processor
2 cups flour
1/2 teaspoon baking powder
2 teaspoons baking soda
1 teaspoon salt
2 to 3 teaspoons cinnamon
1 cup coarsely chopped walnuts
2 teaspoons vanilla

Blend oil, sugar and eggs. Add zucchini. Sift dry ingredients together and add to zucchini mixture. Stir in nuts. Add vanilla and mix well. Pour into 2 lightly greased loaf pans or 1 Bundt pan. Bake 50 to 60 minutes at 350°. Cool 10 minutes before removing from pans.

Hint: Cheryl suggests that when zucchini is plentiful, you should freeze it in 2-cup portions. Then you can defrost it any time of the year to bake this tasty bread.

Tony and Vince (two youngest sons), circa 1936.

Tomato Pick Up

Hot or cold, as a drink or a soup, this simple beverage is a real friend on picnics, at football games, or on car trips. A *Meet Delicato* reader, Sarah Turner, says she puts a smoked sausage in the thermos, fills it with the hot liquid, and when she's ready to eat, she has hot soup and a cooked sausage!

3 cups tomato juice
3 whole cloves
1 tablespoon lemon juice
1-1/2 teaspoons sugar
Salt and pepper to taste
3/4 cup California dry white wine

Combine all ingredients. Heat, but do not boil. Drink hot, or store in refrigerator to drink cold or reheat later. Serves 6.

California Onion Soup

A delicate, cream-colored soup with a mild onion flavor. Everyone who tastes it will ask for the recipe.

3 large yellow onions, thinly sliced (about 6 cups)
6 tablespoons butter
3 cans chicken broth (14-1/2 ounces each)
1-1/2 cups Delicato Chablis Blanc
Salt and pepper
6 slices French bread
1-1/2 cups coarsely grated Swiss cheese

Sauté onions in butter until soft and transparent. Be careful to avoid browning. Add broth and simmer until it is reduced by one-third. Add wine, salt and pepper. Bring to a boil once more and simmer for 10 minutes. Lightly toast 1-inch thick slices of French bread. Place one in each soup bowl. Top with 1/4 cup grated Swiss cheese. Ladle steaming soup over both. Serves 4 to 6.

Serve with Cheesey French Loaf (page 120) for a light lunch. A good soup choice to introduce Baked Ham In Wine (page 110).

Wine Suggestion: California burgundy.

The Indelicato and Luppino families were making a living on the land until Prohibition ended in 1933. Then customers in the East no longer needed grapes for home winemaking. Dad couldn't even get five dollars a ton for them.

There were other small vineyards around us, owned mostly by Italian immigrants, too. When things got tough, a lot of the farmers plowed under their vines and planted other crops or left the area. Some of our neighbors had tanks they weren't using and one day Dad and Uncle said, "Let's make wine!"

Papa during the depression. He thought the ranch was lost.

Spinach Soup

Your guests will love this interesting soup, even if they don't believe the main ingredient is spinach.

1/2 pound fresh spinach or 1 package frozen spinach, thawed
1 tablespoon vegetable oil
2 tablespoons finely minced fresh ginger
2 green onions, chopped, including some greens
2 cans chicken broth (14-1/2 ounces each)
1/4 cup California dry sherry
2 teaspoons soy sauce
1/4 cup sour cream
Sour cream for garnish

Wash spinach and strip from stems. Heat oil. Sauté ginger for about 1 minute. Add spinach and onions, stirring 2 to 3 minutes. Add broth, sherry and soy sauce. Bring to a boil, then simmer for 10 minutes.

Purée with 1/4 cup sour cream. Chill thoroughly or serve hot. Stir well before serving. Garnish with a dollop of sour cream. Makes 4 petite servings or 2 meal-size portions.

Serve with Spoon Bread.

Wine Suggestion: California Chenin Blanc.

Spoon Bread

3 eggs, separated
3 cups milk
1 cup yellow or white cornmeal
1 cup milk
1 teaspoon salt
1 teaspoon baking powder
1 tablespoon butter
1 teaspoon lard or shortening

Beat egg whites until stiff and set aside. In large pan, scald 3 cups milk. In a bowl, mix cornmeal with 1 cup cold milk and stir into scalded milk. Continue heating over medium heat, stirring constantly. Stir yolks into cornmeal mixture. When mixture thickens, *remove from heat* and add salt, baking powder, and butter. Fold in egg whites.

Grease 2-quart casserole with lard or shortening. Pour in mixture and bake at 350° for 50 minutes or until browned on top. Serve immediately. Serves 4 to 6.

Angelo Rolleri, who knew Gaspare Indelicato and his family, came from Italy in 1914. Four years later he opened Genova Bakery to make bread the European way. Today, the bread is still rolled by hand and baked to golden crispness in the specially built brick oven.

Special occasions in the Stockton area call for Genova bread on the table. At the Indelicato family sausage making evenings, there are always plenty of loaves.

As Angelo grew older, he turned the breadmaking over to younger bakers. But he still sat every day in the same spot, on an old wine box, greeting regular customers and neighbors until his death in 1985.

Angelo Rolleri of Genova Bakery.

Pear And Celery Soup

Guests guess the taste of celery in this soup, but are pleasantly surprised by the pears. Together, they create an unusual, tasty, cold, summer soup.

2-3/4 cups finely chopped celery
2 cans chicken broth (14-1/2 ounces each)
1 cup peeled, chopped Bartlett pear
1/3 cup Delicato Chardonnay
2 tablespoons heavy cream
Nutmeg

Simmer celery and broth uncovered for about 20 minutes, or until celery is soft. Drain and purée celery and pear in blender, gradually adding hot broth. Add wine. Chill.

At serving time, stir well and ladle into serving bowls. Carefully top with cream and a grating of nutmeg. Serves 6.

Accompany with popovers. Move on to Peppery Kebabs (page 96), Vegetable Kebabs (page 122), and Spanish Basque Flan (page 132) for a wonderful meal all within the pages of this book.

Wine Suggestion: Gerwurztraminer or Delicato Chardonnay.

Apple-Lemon Soup

Wonderful fresh-apple flavor with a texture like delicate apple sauce.

5 to 6 medium apples (1-1/2 pounds)
1 cinnamon stick
Rind of 1 lemon, cut into strips
3 tablespoons cornstarch
1/2 cup water
1/4 cup sugar
1/2 teaspoon salt
1/2 cup Delicato Green Hungarian
Sour cream

Core apples and cut each into 6 pieces. Place in deep kettle with 1-1/2 quarts water, cinnamon stick, and lemon rind. Cook over low heat until apples are very soft. Remove cinnamon and purée lemon rind and apples with liquid. Return to kettle.

Blend cornstarch in water and stir into soup. Cook over low heat until thickened and smooth, stirring constantly. Add sugar, salt and wine. Serve hot or cold with a dollop of sour cream. Serves 6.

Wine Suggestion: California Green Hungarian or Gewürztraminer.

ROYAL BURGUNDY

1 teaspoon cherry liqueur
1 teaspoon lemon juice
1 teaspoon powdered sugar
2/3 cup California burgundy
Cracked ice
Fresh fruit

Make a syrup by mixing liqueur, juice and sugar in a tall glass. Add burgundy and cracked ice. Garnish with fruit. Makes a single serving.

Salads

Little Caesar Salad

A zippy salad to serve with pizza or pasta.

1 large bunch broccoli
1 large head Romaine lettuce
1/2 cup olive oil
1/3 cup Delicato Chablis Blanc
2 tablespoons white wine vinegar
1/2 teaspoon salt
Freshly ground pepper
1/4 teaspoon Worcestershire sauce
Dash paprika
1/3 cup grated Parmesan cheese
1 minced garlic clove
1 raw egg yolk
Minced anchovies (optional)

Wash broccoli, removing flowerettes and chopping thin stems into 1/2-inch pieces. Use thick stalks for other purposes. Steam until *al dente*. Cool.

Wash and dry Romaine leaves. Wrap loosely in paper towels if salad will not be prepared immediately.

Combine remaining ingredients, except egg yolk and anchovies, in mixing bowl and beat until well blended. Pour slowly over lettuce and broccoli, stopping when mixture is moist, not soaking. (You may have more dressing then is necessary for this salad. Use the rest on another salad or as a marinade for meat or chicken.) Toss lightly. Drop in egg yolk and mix well. Add anchovies, if desired.

If dressing will not be used immediately, store in covered container in refrigerator and beat well just before serving. Serves 4 as meal-size salads, or 6 as dinner salads.

Wine Suggestion: California burgundy or Zinfandel.

In 1924 Dad and Uncle Sam Luppino planted small plots of Carignane, Mission and Zinfandel grapes for making their own wine. They also sold grapes to the East Coast for family winemaking.

The walnut trees were planted at the ends of the vineyards so Dad and Uncle had a shady place to rest the horses. Just recently when we planted new vines we knew it would be practical to uproot the trees and make room for additional vines. But we all decided we needed these trees for sentiment's sake. It was here under these trees that Dad and Uncle sat and drilled each other in English. Dad was determined to learn English. One of his favorite stories was of when he went before the judge to receive his citizenship. "The judge asked the questions and I answered right back. The judge said nice words about my answers," he remembered proudly.

Tossed Spinach Salad

This crisp and fresh salad goes with so many entrées. Also, delicious as a luncheon salad.

8 water chestnuts, thinly sliced
3 hard-cooked eggs, thinly sliced
3 slices bacon, finely crumbled
1/4 cup salad oil
1 tablespoon sugar
1 tablespoon catsup
1 tablespoon white wine vinegar
1/2 teaspoon Worcestershire sauce
2 teaspoons California dry sherry
1 large bunch spinach
2 green onions, coarsely chopped, including some greens
3 cups bean sprouts
Black pepper to taste

If you have time, crispen chestnuts by draining water from can and refilling with tap water mixed with 1 teaspoon sugar. Refrigerate until using. Keep unused chestnuts in sugar solution until needed.

Boil eggs until hard-cooked. Cool and set aside.

Fry bacon slices until crisp. Drain on absorbent paper. Crumble or cut into small pieces. Set aside.

Combine oil, sugar, catsup, vinegar, Worcestershire sauce and sherry. Shake well in jar.

Wash spinach and destem. Dry with towel or spin dry. Place in large bowl. Add onions and bean sprouts. Toss lightly but well.

Add dressing and toss again. Season with pepper to taste. Slice eggs and lay on top. Serve immediately. Makes 6 accompanying salads or 2 to 3 entrée salads.

Wine Suggestion: California Rosé of Cabernet.

Oriental Chicken Salad

GLISTENING RICE

2 cups boiling water
1 cup rice
1/4 cup white vinegar
3 teaspoons sugar
1/2 teaspoon salt

Add rice to boiling water. Bring to boil and stir. Reduce heat to lowest flame and cover pot. Cook without lifting lid for 20 minutes. Turn off heat and let sit for 5 minutes.

Place hot rice in bowl. Combine vinegar, sugar, and salt and pour mixture over rice. Stir thoroughly. Let cool to room temperature. Cover and chill.

At serving time, pack rice into small bowls (about 1/2 cup capacity). Unmold on center of individual plates. Arrange salad around mound. Serves 4.

This salad has several preparation stages, but the beautiful blend of flavors makes it all worthwhile. Most of this salad can be prepared the day before, and the chilled ingredients assembled in minutes just before serving. The result is an exotic, fresh salad.

2 chicken breasts, or 2 cups chicken meat
Chicken Marinade
1 cup walnut pieces
Dash salt
1 teaspoon curry powder
12 ounces Chinese pea pods
3 cups watercress, without stems
Salad Dressing
Glistening Rice

CHICKEN MARINADE:

1/3 cup soy sauce
1/3 cup California dry sherry
4 garlic cloves
4 thin slices fresh ginger

Marinate chicken 1 to 2 hours at room temperature. Broil until done and skin is crisp. Slice meat into thin strips. Reserve and chill.

WALNUTS:

Place nuts on cookie sheet or tin foil in 300° oven. Sprinkle with salt and 1 teaspoon curry powder. Toast until crisp and lightly brown. Cool nuts for at least an hour, allowing them to become crisp before adding to salad.

PEA PODS:

Rinse pods and remove strings. Blanch in boiling water for 2 to 3 minutes until just barely cooked. Submerge immediately in ice water to retain crispness. Drain and chill.

WATERCRESS:

Wash watercress. Remove thick stems. Divide into small sprigs but do not cut or mince. Shake dry and wrap in cloth or paper towel. Refrigerate.

SALAD DRESSING:

5 tablespoons peanut oil
3 tablespoons white vinegar
1/2 teaspoon mild curry powder

Mix thoroughly and reserve. Shake well before adding to salad minutes before serving.

SERVING:

At serving time combine watercress, pea pods, chicken and nuts. Toss well. Add salad dressing and toss lightly. Surround Glistening Rice with salad.

Wine Suggestion: California Delicato Green Hungarian.

Scallop Salad

A delicate crunch of cucumber and nuts plus summer colors of pink and green. Gorgeous presented in a clear glass bowl.

1 cup California dry white wine
Bouquet garni of 1/4 teaspoon thyme, 2 sprigs parsley,
   2 pieces green onion (1 inch long), 1 bay leaf
1 pound bay scallops (the tiny ones)
6 tablespoons grapeseed oil
1 tablespoon white wine vinegar
1/4 teaspoon mustard
8 tablespoons peeled, finely minced cucumber
4 tablespoons minced pistachios
Dash chervil
Salt to taste
Bibb lettuce or watercress
Lime wedges

Gaspare and Caterina, 1931.

Bring wine to a simmer, add *bouquet garni* and poach scallops for 5 minutes. Cool. Remove scallops from liquid.

Mix grapeseed oil, vinegar and mustard. Marinate scallops in mixture at room temperature for at least 2 hours.

At serving time, add cucumber, pistachios, chervil and salt, and mix well.

Serve in a single Bibb lettuce leaf or in a nest of watercress. Add 2 lime wedges for each serving. Makes 4 ample appetizer or salad servings.

Wine Suggestion: California White Zinfandel.

Minted Tomato Salad

An easy to prepare tomato salad with plenty of refreshing mint.

SALAD DRESSING:

4 tablespoons olive oil
2 tablespoons California dry white wine
1 teaspoon lemon juice
Freshly ground black pepper
Dash cayenne pepper
Pinch sugar
Pinch dry mustard
1 clove garlic, crushed

Blend all ingredients. Chill before using. Remove garlic clove before serving or after an hour of chilling.

SALAD:

6 firm tomatoes, skinned and sliced
1 medium onion, thinly sliced
1 cup fresh mint leaves, finely minced
Salad dressing
Romaine lettuce

Combine tomatoes, onions and mint in a bowl. Pour dressing over and toss lightly. Serve on crisp lettuce leaves. Delicious with grilled lamb. Serves 6 or 8 as an accompanying salad.

Wine Suggestion: California Zinfandel or Petite Sirah.

French Potato Salad

A light salad resplendent of tarragon.

6 medium potatoes
1/8 teaspoon salt
1/8 teaspoon freshly ground pepper
3 tablespoons tarragon or white wine vinegar*
2 tablespoons chicken broth
2 tablespoons California dry white wine
1 teaspoon dried tarragon
1 tablespoon fresh parsley
3 tablespoons salad oil (not olive oil)

Cook potatoes in salt water for 30 minutes or until tender. Peel while still warm and cut into slices approximately 1/4-inch thick. Place in bowl.

In smaller bowl, combine salt, pepper, vinegar, broth and wine. Mix until salt is dissolved. Add tarragon and parsley. Whisk in oil. Pour over warm potatoes. Toss gently until all liquid is absorbed. Serve while warm. Makes 4 to 6 servings.

This dish is a natural contribution to a picnic. Delicious with sweet and sour carrots, pumpernickel bread, and corned beef.

Hint: Potatoes should absorb the flavorings while they are still warm—otherwise they get a "cold potato" taste which overpowers the delicate dressing.

Wine Suggestion: California Sauvignon blanc.

Do not use red wine vinegar. If using plain cider or white wine vinegar without tarragon, increase dried tarragon by 1/4 teaspoon.

Vacations were almost unheard of for a large family like ours in the Depression days, but we did have a chance to go camping near Chico, at Richardson Springs. We had very little money to spend, just enough for the gas to get there.

There were seven of us in a 1935 Chevy. People used to count in disbelief as we got out of that small car, one by one.

Because we had no cash for groceries, we took along our food, including a crate of live chickens. We must have made quite a sight—all packed in the car like sardines, and those squawking chickens tied on the back. When we got there, they crowed at sunrise and woke up our family and everyone else.

Chick Pea Salad

In May 1935, the winery officially opened. Proud to be in business in this new land, Dad and Uncle, partners in this new venture, Americanized their names: Sebastiano became Sam, and Gaspare changed to Jasper. They called their venture the Sam Jasper Winery.

The winery's first vintage, 3,411 gallons, was made in a converted hay barn, using a small hand crusher and a hand-operated winepress. Local people, mostly Italians, bought the red wine that first year for 50 cents a gallon.

We did everything ourselves—growing the grapes, making the wine and selling it.

This is a recipe from Joe Larrañaga, Delicato employee for 25 years. Joe recommends this bean dish either as a salad or as a side dish with meat, fish or chicken. "The Basques make a fine sandwich of these beans and French bread," Joe adds.

1 pound dried garbanzo beans
1 teaspoon salt
1 medium onion, minced
2 cloves garlic, minced
2 tablespoons tomato sauce
1 tablespoon olive oil

Wash the garbanzos and put them in a deep kettle with salt and enough water to cover. Soak overnight. Add more water if necessary to cover beans completely.

Bring to a boil, skimming off foam 3 or 4 times until water is clear. Add minced onion and garlic, tomato sauce and oil. Cover and simmer for 3 hours. Refrain from stirring beans, but check often to maintain enough liquid. Makes four dinner or eight salad portions.

Wine Suggestion: California Cabernet Sauvignon.

Original winery building.

Basic Vinaigrette

Also called basic French dressing. The usual proportion of vinegar to oil is 1 to 3, but you may want to discover your own ratio.

1/2 cup olive oil
2 tablespoons red wine vinegar
2 tablespoons Zinfandel
1/2 teaspoon salt
Freshly ground black pepper

Put ingredients in a small bowl. Stir until salt dissolves.

Hints: For all green salads, be certain leaves are completely dry so dressing will adhere. Toss salad just before serving time and only enough to coat the leaves. There should be no pool of dressing left in the bottom of the bowl.

ADDITIONS TO BASIC VINAIGRETTE:

1. Add 1/2 teaspoon mustard, 1/2 teaspoon Worcestershire sauce and 1 minced clove garlic.

2. Add 3 teaspoons chopped anchovies, 1-1/2 teaspoons chopped capers, 2 teaspoons chopped parsley and 4 drops Tabasco sauce.

3. Add 1 teaspoon sugar and a pinch *each* of dried basil and tarragon.

4. Add 3 tablespoons chutney, 2 teaspoons walnut catsup and 1 tablespoon dried chervil.

5. Add 1/4 cup total combination or single selection of fresh herbs: marjoram, rosemary, tarragon, chervil, chives or savory.

Vineyard Vinaigrette

William (Bill) Nakata, Vice President in charge of Plant Operations, shares this recipe.

6 tablespoons grapeseed oil
3 tablespoons red wine vinegar
1 tablespoon honey
1 clove garlic, peeled and crushed
1/8 teaspoon tarragon
1/8 teaspoon basil
1/8 teaspoon oregano

Mix all ingredients together thoroughly. Let sit at least 30 minutes, removing garlic at that time if dressing will be stored longer. Shake well before pouring over lettuce greens. Makes approximately 1/2 cup dressing.

White Wine Dressing

A light dressing for salad greens or summer pasta salads.

6 tablespoons olive oil
2 tablespoons Delicato Chablis Blanc
1/2 teaspoon lemon juice (optional)
1/2 teaspoon salt
Freshly ground pepper
Dash cayenne pepper
Pinch sugar
Pinch dry mustard
Slice mild onion

Blend ingredients together and let rest for at least 30 minutes. Remove onion slice before serving.

Pasta

Tips For The Best Pasta

Pasta is more than spaghetti—pasta comes in rings, shells, strands, elbows, tubes—even mustache shapes! Team up any of these with pasta sauces for an exciting new dinner time combination.

Allow 4 ounces of dried pasta for each guest. Serve cooked pasta in a large bowl in the center of the table or dish up individual portions from the head of the table.

Place bowls of freshly grated Parmesan or Romano cheeses, sweet butter, minced parsley and green onions, grated walnuts, pesto, and anchovies on the table. Diners can spice up sauces with these condiments or create their own flavor combinations.

Red Or White Wine With Pasta?

If your pasta sauce is abundantly flavored with garlic, herbs and tomato, try a hearty red wine such as Zinfandel or Petite Sirah. If your sauce is more delicate or you prefer white wine, serve a full-bodied white, either Chardonnay or Sauvignon blanc.

For The Best Possible Pasta:

- Cook in plenty of water. Use 3 quarts of water for each 8 ounces of dried pasta (two average servings). Bring water to a rolling boil. Slowly add pasta. Bring to a second boil, and simmer until done.
- Do not overcook. Chefs agree that the cooking times given on pasta packages are too long. Pasta tastes best *al dente* (tender but firm "to the tooth"). Spaghetti is well-cooked in 12 minutes, and smaller pasta pieces even faster. Taste a piece as cooking time nears 10 minutes.
- Do not rinse cooked pasta. Pasta has a better texture if it is not rinsed. Lift pasta directly from cooking water to serving plate or bowl with a pasta fork or other utensil. Drain smaller pasta in a colander.

Keep plenty of pasta in your cupboard and sauce in your freezer, and you'll always have quick, tasty meals near at hand.

Anchovy Sauce

1/4 cup olive oil
4 tablespoons butter
4 garlic cloves, minced
1 can anchovies (2 ounces) drained and minced
1/4 cup California dry white wine
1/3 cup minced parsley

Heat olive oil and butter. Add garlic and cook over low heat until garlic is soft but not brown. Add anchovies and wine and mix well. Stir until anchovies blend into the sauce. Stir in parsley and serve immediately over hot pasta. Makes about 3/4 cup sauce.

Today's Tomato Sauce

We name this recipe "today's tomato sauce" because it shows a change from the original recipe which called for home canned tomatoes grown in the garden. "Now we use commercially canned tomato sauce, but cook it the same way," says Frances, who believes that 30 minutes is the most time needed to simmer a sauce.

This basic sauce is delicious over pasta and adds flavors by the spoonful to other sauces.

"A good addition to this sauce is made by carefully breaking a couple of whole eggs into the simmering sauce. Don't stir," Frances cautions, "and be sure to cover the pot or the eggs will stick to the bottom of the pan. Simmer for 5 minutes, or until eggs are cooked, over very low heat and pour over pasta."

Frances remembers, too, when a whole head of garlic would be dropped in the sauce and cooked until soft. In Italian the garlic was called a "lamb's head" and would be divided between the servings.

"Or, if you like a thick sauce," Frances says, "put a cut-up, raw potato in the sauce and cook it until it is done."

Olive oil
3/4 cup finely minced onions
4 cloves garlic, minced
3 cans tomato sauce (8 ounces each)
Salt and pepper to taste
Bay leaf

Brown onions and garlic in olive oil. Add tomato sauce, bay leaf and salt and pepper. Simmer for 30 minutes.

Caterina's Pasta Ascuitta

CATERINA'S SUNDAY NIGHT PASTA ASCUITTA

"Every Sunday night we ate *Pasta Ascuitta,* which means pasta with sauce. The pasta could be any shape— whatever Mom bought at the Italian grocery in town but the sauce was usually the same. We ate as much as our stomachs could hold. It was contentment. We could even forget we had to go to school the next day."

—Frank Indelicato

All four Indelicato children remember the good pasta with sauce that the family ate every Sunday night. Frances, because she cooked alongside her Mom, remembers how it was prepared. Today, Frances sometimes substitutes beef for poultry. "Just be sure the beef is cooked through before adding the other ingredients," she advises.

Olive oil for frying
1 rabbit or chicken, cut up into small pieces
3 garlic cloves, minced
3/4 cup minced onion
Salt and pepper to taste
1 can whole tomatoes with juice (28 ounces)
2 cans tomato sauce (8 ounces each)
1 can tomato paste (2 ounces)
1/4 cup minced parsley
Fresh sweet basil to taste, minced
Pasta (Spaghetti, Linguini, Mostaccioli or your choice)
Grated Romano cheese

In a 6 to 8 quart saucepan heat olive oil. Brown chicken or rabbit pieces for about 20 minutes with lid on. Add garlic, onion and salt and pepper and simmer covered for 10 to 15 minutes. Add tomatoes, tomato sauce and paste, parsley and basil. Simmer covered for 45 minutes.

Serve hot over cooked pasta. Place a bowl of grated cheese on the table so people can sprinkle some on top. This recipe will feed 4 to 8, depending on the size of appetites. It can easily be expanded by adding another can of tomatoes and cutting poultry into smaller pieces.

Sciabica's Pasta Topping

Joe Sciabica fixes up a batch of this pasta topping for himself and son, Joe, Jr. when their wives, Frances and Laurie are gone for the evening. Joe doesn't worry too much about the ratio of ingredients. "It's how you want it—and all you want!"

1/2 cup bread crumbs*
1 or 2 garlic cloves, minced
3 leaves sweet basil, minced
3 sprigs parsley, finely minced
2 tablespoons Romano or Parmesan cheese
1 tablespoon olive oil
1/4 pound pasta of your choice

Mix bread crumbs, garlic, basil, parsley and cheese. Blend in olive oil and mix well. Place mixed bread crumbs in heavy skillet over low heat. Stir constantly with wooden spoon so mixture will not burn. When crumbs are toasted, remove from heat.

In a separate pot cook pasta. Drain the pasta but reserve about 1/4 cup of cooking water. Return it to the pasta so it won't be dry. Add the toasted bread crumbs and toss lightly. Sprinkle cheese on top—and dig in! Makes two people very content.

*Joe says, "I make my own bread crumbs from hard French bread. Or, if I don't have bread on hand, I use Progresso Bread Crumbs Italian-Style and simply add the olive oil."

Joe Sciabica, Sr., son-in-law of founder, enjoying his wine, 1985.

Mushroom Sauce

1-1/2 pounds mushrooms, very thinly sliced
1/2 cup butter
2/3 cup California dry white wine
1 garlic clove, crushed
1/2 cup minced parsley
6 ounces cooked pasta
Black pepper, freshly ground

Sauté mushrooms in butter in shallow skillet until they are golden and the mushroom liquid disappears (about 20 minutes).

Add wine and garlic and simmer, occasionally stirring. When wine is almost completely gone, remove from heat and add parsley. Add cooked, hot pasta and toss together. Grind black pepper over all. Makes 2 dinner servings or 4 first-course servings.

Spaghetti And Ragú

"The children went to the winery with me in the morning. Around 9:30, the time Nanna Indelicato usually ate breakfast, the children went next door to see her and have a second breakfast. After the second breakfast they would then come back to the winery with me. Robert, now in his twenties and working at the winery as Assistant Sales Manager, still remembers how Nanna cooked the eggs fresh from the backyard chickens. They were soft, he recalls, and he and his sister dipped their French bread into them. No eggs have ever tasted as good since, they claim.

"After breakfast with Nanna, the children joined me in the office, sometimes playing under my desk, crouching by my feet. When they were older they told me how they'd stay quiet and watch the feet on the other side of the desk when I had a visitor.

"I often prepare pasta because Vince enjoys it so much. When the children were young they were always hungry and couldn't wait for dinner. I could satisfy them temporarily by dipping pieces of French bread in the simmering sauce. They still talk about my good before-dinner snacks."

—Dorothy Indelicato

1 pound lean ground beef
1/2 cup finely minced onion
2 cloves garlic, minced
5 cans tomato sauce (8 ounces each)
1 sprig fresh rosemary (or 1/4 teaspoon dried)
1 tablespoon fresh, minced parsley
1/2 teaspoon thyme
1 large bay leaf
1 teaspoon dried oregano
1/2 cup Delicato Zinfandel
Salt
Mushrooms (optional)
4 ounces spaghetti per serving

Brown beef in skillet until almost cooked. Leave about 2 tablespoons fat in pan with meat. Sauté onions and garlic until limp. Add tomato sauce, mushrooms, herbs and wine. Salt to taste. Stir well. Bring to a boil. Turn heat down to simmer. Cook at least 30 minutes, an hour if you have the time. Makes enough sauce for 8 servings.

Vermicelli With Mint

Begin a summer meal with small portions of the pasta. Follow with Roast Chicken (page 77) and Red Pepper Gratin (page 119).

3 tablespoons butter
2 cloves garlic, crushed
1/2 pound mild Italian sausage
1/2 cup California dry white wine
1 cup finely chopped fresh mint
1 teaspoon dried oregano
Salt
1 pound vermicelli

In a medium skillet, melt butter, add garlic and sauté until golden. Remove sausage meat from casings, crumble and sauté until brown. Remove garlic. Add wine, mint and oregano. Salt to taste. Cover and simmer for 5 minutes. Turn off heat and let stand.

Cook vermicelli until *al dente*. Drain well and place in large serving bowl. Add sauce and mix well. Serve immediately in soup bowls. Serves 4 as a meal, or 8 as a first course.

Winter Vegetable Sauce

6 tablespoons olive oil
1 dried red chili pepper (use less for a milder sauce)
2 cloves garlic, minced
1 can Italian plum tomatoes (28 ounces)
Salt to taste
1 teaspoon dried basil
3 bay leaves
2 cups broccoli flowerettes, steamed *al dente*
2 cups cauliflower flowerettes, steamed *al dente*
1/2 cup California dry sherry

In a large skillet, heat oil and sauté chili pepper and garlic until lightly golden. Squeeze or crush tomatoes by hand and add them with salt, basil and bay leaves to the skillet. Mix well, cover and cook for 20 minutes over moderate heat. Add vegetables and sherry. Cover and simmer for 5 minutes. Turn off flame, remove bay leaves and chili pepper and let stand while pasta cooks. Heat up quickly before serving. Makes 4 dinner portions or 6 side dish portions.

Pesto For Pasta

When basil is abundant in the summer, make up a year's supply to keep in your freezer. No need to wash blender between batches.

2 cups basil leaves without stems, washed and dried
1 tablespoon minced garlic (about 6 cloves)
1/2 cup good quality olive oil
3/4 cup grated Parmesan or Romano cheese (about 3 ounces)
2 tablespoons pine nuts

Place basil leaves, garlic, oil, cheese and pine nuts in blender and grate or chop until leaves are blended. Scrape down sides and purée until mixture is thoroughly blended. Scrape sides down again and check for any unblended garlic. Continue to blend until mixture is smooth. At this point the mixture will be bright green and look somewhat curdled.

If not using pesto immediately, place 1 tablespoon of mixture into an ice cube square. Cover tray with plastic wrap and freeze. When solid, unmold cubes and place in small baggie or wrap individually in foil or plastic wrap. This recipe makes 8 or 9 cubes.

RED OR WHITE WINE WITH PASTA?

If your pasta sauce is abundantly flavored with garlic, herbs and tomato, try a hearty red wine such as Zinfandel or Petite Sirah. If your sauce is more delicate or you prefer white wine, serve a full-bodied white, either Chardonnay or Sauvignon blanc.

Shells and Zucchini

3 medium zucchini
1 carrot, coarsely chopped
1 yellow onion, coarsely chopped
3 tablespoons olive oil
1/2 teaspoon oregano
1 tablespoon fresh basil (or 1/2 teaspoon dried)
2 tablespoons marinara sauce
1 can chicken broth (14-1/2 ounces)
1/2 cup California dry white wine
1/2 cup grated Parmesan cheese
1 cup small macaroni shells

Partially peel washed zucchini, leaving some green skin for color. Remove a thick slice from each end and quarter zucchini lengthwise. Cut zucchini into 1/4-inch slices. Chop carrots and onions into small pieces.

In a large pan or Dutch oven, heat oil and sauté carrots and onions until onion is golden. Add zucchini, oregano, basil and marinara sauce. Mix well and stir for a few minutes. Add broth and wine. Cover and simmer for a few minutes. Bring to a boil, stirring in cheese. Simmer for 15 minutes. Season to taste.

Cook macaroni shells until *al dente*. Drain and add to other ingredients. Stir well, and simmer for 5 minutes. Serve in soup bowls with additional cheese sprinkled over individual servings. Makes 6 side dish or 4 dinner servings.

Garlic Pasta Sauce

This sauce always disappears first at a pasta party. Serve it in a small gravy boat, explaining to guests that a little goes a long way.

1/2 cup garlic, peeled and finely minced
1/2 cup butter
1/2 cup olive oil
1 cup parsley, finely minced

Cook garlic in butter and oil over medium heat until soft but not browned. Lower heat and simmer for at least one hour. Add parsley and cook, stirring for 1 to 2 minutes until limp. Serve immediately.

Seafood

Delta Catfish With Garlic

"We remember the Busalacchis, for it was Frank's father who saved the Indelicato property from foreclosure.

"Times were so tough during the Depression that dad couldn't even make the interest payments on the land. It looked as if there was no way out. When the Busalacchis learned of our trouble, they went to a friend at the bank and pleaded for an extension on the loan. Without that favor, there would be no winery here."

—Frank, Tony and Vince
Indelicato

"We met Gaspare in Lodi a long time ago—we're both in our eighties now—where we all worked harvesting grapes. In 1921 we attended the double wedding of Caterina and her twin sister, Serafina, to Gaspare Indelicato and Sebastiano Luppino.

"When we got married in 1927, Caterina and Gaspare were at the wedding. The painting of a sunset over a lake—maybe it's in Italy—that hangs over our dining room buffet was the Indelicato gift to us. It's been there since we moved into this house after our honeymoon.

"We were friends for a long time. We'd drive out to visit them on Sundays. In summer Gaspare would send us to the watermelon patch where we'd eat as much as we wanted. When it was time to go home, he'd load us up with whatever he had—a box of grapes or a sack of vegetables.

"We remember Gaspare coming into Stockton on Wednesdays and Fridays in his old truck to sell wine. He'd come by our fish market to deliver wine. We usually sent fish home for his family. He'd take plenty of scraps, for Caterina made a fine fish head soup.

"They were poor people. They had nothing materially, but they were happy on the land and always shared with others. If Gaspare were here today he wouldn't believe how the winery has grown and how well his children have done. He'd be proud."

—Mary and Frank Busalacchi

Busalacchi Fish Market.

Delta Catfish With Garlic

"We've been cooking our fish like this for years. It's simple and so good," says Frank Busalacchi, who met Gaspare Indelicato in the early 1920's when they both worked in Lodi-area vineyards. "I wish I could say we used wine to cook it, but we don't. We save all the wine to drink *with the fish.*"

1 catfish (about 8 ounces) skinned, cleaned with head and tail removed*
2 tablespoons olive oil
3 cloves garlic, minced (about 1 tablespoon)
2 tablespoons minced parsley
1 tablespoon fresh basil, minced *or* 1/2 teaspoon dried basil
1/2 cup hot water
Salt and pepper to taste
2 tablespoons Romano or Parmesan cheese

Sauté garlic in olive oil until limp and lightly tinged with brown. Add fish and sauté until browned, turning once. Another tablespoon of oil may be needed.

Add parsley, basil and hot water. Season to taste. Cover and reduce heat. Simmer for 10 to 15 minutes, or until fish is cooked through. Check occasionally for liquid in pan.

Remove fish to heated serving plate. Stir remaining liquid with garlic/herb pieces and pour over fish. Sprinkle cheese on top. Makes a single portion.

Wine Suggestion: California Petite Sirah or Zinfandel.

**Rock cod or sole fillets may be substituted.*

Filleting fish, circa 1929.

Sumptuous Snapper

Prepare at the last minute. The sauce goes well on chicken and ham, too.

4 thin red snapper fillets (3 to 4 ounces each)
Flour for dredging
1 tablespoon olive oil
1 tablespoon butter
1 tablespoon Country Style Dijon mustard (with seeds)
2 tablespoons California dry white wine
1/2 cup heavy cream
1 tablespoon butter
Salt and pepper to taste

Melt oil and butter in skillet. Lightly dredge fish fillets in flour. Sauté over medium heat about 3 minutes on each side, turning only once. Remove to warm serving plate and keep hot.

In smaller pan, blend mustard and wine over medium-high heat for 1 minute. Reduce heat, add cream, whisking while reducing sauce by one-fourth. Remove pan from heat, whisk in butter, season to taste and pour over hot fish. Serve at once. Serves 2 to 3.

Wine Suggestion: California Chardonnay.

Baked Perch

Cheese and bread crumbs bubble together atop perch fillets.

1 tablespoon butter
2 pounds perch fillets
4 shallots, minced
3 tablespoons butter
Salt and pepper to taste
1 cup California dry white wine, heated
1/2 cup fresh bread crumbs
3/4 cup Swiss cheese, grated

Preheat oven to 400°. Place fillets in buttered baking dish. Add shallots and dot with remaining butter. Season with salt and pepper. Cover fish with heated wine and bake for 15 minutes, or until done. Remove dish from oven and sprinkle with crumbs and grated cheese. Brown under broiler until lightly browned and bubbly. Serve immediately. Serves 6.

Wine Suggestion: California Sauvignon blanc or Zinfandel.

Grilled Whole Trout

Sea and orchard come together with a light touch of orange.

1 whole trout per person

MARINADE:

1 cup Delicato Chablis Blanc
1 tablespoon grated orange rind
8 bay leaves, broken
6 peppercorns, crushed
1/4 cup fresh orange juice
2 tablespoons olive oil

Marinate fish in glass dish at room temperature for 1 hour. Grill over hot mesquite charcoal until flesh is flaky, turning fish once. Serve immediately with lemon wedges.

Wine Suggestion: Gewürztraminer.

Spirited Sole

A soul-satisfying fish dish simmered in wine.

Butter for greasing dish
1 pound sole fillets (or other firm white fish)
2 green onions, chopped, including greens
1/2 cup Delicato Chablis Blanc
Water as needed (or more wine, if you wish)
1 tablespoon butter
1 tablespoon flour
Salt and pepper to taste
Cayenne pepper
1/4 cup ripe olives, thinly sliced
Parsley for garnish

Put fillets in greased skillet or shallow baking dish. Sprinkle onions on top and in between fish pieces. Pour wine over fillets. Simmer 10 to 15 minutes, covered. When fish is flaky, remove fillets to heated platter and reserve liquid.

Melt butter and blend in flour, making a smooth paste. Add strained fish poaching liquid, salt, pepper and desired amount of cayenne, stirring until a medium-thick sauce is achieved. Add olives and parsley and pour over fish. Makes 3 or 4 servings.

Wine Suggestion: California burgundy.

In 1944 Frances got engaged to Joe Sciabica, whose mother came from the same town in Sicily as Dad. Everyone still talks about the engagement party that hot summer day. Joe butchered an 800-pound steer and cut it into steaks. Gaspare made a special grill in the backyard, and 150 family and friends ate meat like they hadn't seen it for fifteen years. We had salads, and fruit and lots of wine and some of the guests who had come from a distance stayed for a visit.

Joe and Frances Sciabica.

Scallop Sauté

The winery grew slowly but steadily. By 1940 a gallon of wine had gone from 50 to 95 cents. Because wine production was limited during the war years, the winery sold all it made, and by 1944 the price soared to $1.90 a gallon. Those profitable times allowed Mom and Dad to build the family brick house and to make their only trip back to Italy.

In the early fifties we three sons joined the business. In 1955 production reached 74,107 gallons—a long way from the 3,411 gallons of twenty years earlier. When Dad passed away in 1962, we were still a small, struggling winery.

At that time Tony was the winemaker, Vince was selling on the road and Frank was cellar manager. Dorothy was hired at 30 dollars a month as the first office clerk. She worked in the unheated office in front of the fermenters and complained of light-headedness from the fumes. It was a big occasion when we finally bought her a used Monroe calculator.

1952 photo. **A** - original sales room. **B** - winery. **C** -papa's garden. **D** - original house that held 10 people. **E** - rabbit hutch. **F** - garage that held 1935 Chevy.

When the rice is almost ready, start the scallops. They'll be done in just five minutes.

1/4 cup olive oil
2 tablespoons coarsely minced shallots
Flour for sautéeing
1 pound bay scallops
3/4 cup Delicato Chardonnay
Steamed rice
Minced parsley for garnish
Lemon wedges

Heat oil in large, shallow skillet. Add shallots and sauté until limp. Lightly flour scallops and add to skillet. Sauté over high heat, shaking pan but not stirring.

Add wine and simmer for several minutes. Serve over rice. Garnish liberally with parsley and accompany with lemon wedges for extra zip. Serves 4.

Precede entrée with hot Spinach Soup (page 43) and conclude with a fruit dessert such as Baked Pears With Ginger Cream (page 128).

Wine Suggestion: California Chardonnay.

Variation: Sauté 1/4 cup thinly sliced mushrooms with scallops. Serve scallops in patty shells for a nice change, too.

Two Trout Dishes

If you have a lot of fish and lots of people to feed, make both sauces. Spoon over fresh trout quickly sautéed in butter.

I.

1 teaspoon anchovy paste
1/4 cup California dry sherry
1 tablespoon lemon juice
1 tablespoon minced parsley
1/2 teaspoon dried mint
1 tablespoon butter
Salt and pepper to taste

Cook anchovy paste, sherry, lemon juice, parsley and mint in butter for 3 to 4 minutes. Taste for seasoning. Stir well and pour over hot fish. Makes enough sauce for 1 large serving. Increase ingredients for additional servings.

II.

1 tablespoon butter
1/4 cup chopped parsley
1 tablespoon minced fresh tarragon (or 1 teaspoon dried tarragon)
1/2 cup California dry white wine

Melt butter. Stir in parsley, tarragon and wine. Cook over high heat for 1 minute, stirring constantly. Pour over hot fish. Makes a single serving. Adjust amount of ingredients to number of servings.

Dad always said he planted a garden but raised kids. He believed in the value of work, so we all did chores every day around the farm. If we ran out of things to do, there were always bottles to wash, for in those days bottles were returnable.

We had been told since we were three-feet high that we'd go to college. Dad often told the story of how he asked his own father in Sicily if he could go to school.

"You want to be a lawyer?" the father asked his son. "No," Gaspare admitted. "I don't want to be a lawyer. I just want to learn." But his father was unconvinced, and when Gaspare left Italy for America, he had only one year of schooling.

Washing jugs on Saturdays and Sundays to prepare for bottling the next day. Two founders on right.

Three Fish Sauces

"Nanna liked snails. Because I was a small child, I remember her as a big lady, even though she was only five feet tall. She was a gentle lady. I remember the days when she'd hand me an empty coffee can and I'd head into the garden to find snails. When I had it filled, she'd give me candy. When she cooked the snails, I ate some, but I remember thinking they were pretty chewy."

—Robert Indelicato

"I remember how the snails got into the family garden in the first place: When Gaspare made trips to San Francisco, he'd stop by the cemeteries and gather snails to bring home. They're prolific creatures and soon we had all we could eat."

—Joe Sciabica

I. MUSTARD SAUCE FOR FISH

Delicious with poached cod or other firm white fish.

1 tablespoon butter
1 tablespoon flour
1 cup bottled clam juice
1/4 teaspoon lemon juice
1 tablespoon very finely minced green onion or shallot
1 teaspoon prepared brown mustard
1-1/2 tablespoons California dry white wine

Melt butter. Blend in flour and cook over low heat for 2 minutes. Gradually add clam juice, stirring until slightly thickened. Combine lemon juice, onion, mustard and wine. Simmer 10 minutes over very low heat. Makes 3/4 cup sauce—enough for 2 ample servings.

II. SWEET AND SOUR SAUCE

This sauce perks up poached cod or is equally good with baked chicken and pork chops.

1-1/2 tablespoons arrowroot or cornstarch
1/2 cup pineapple juice drained from can
1/2 tablespoon soy sauce
1/4 cup white vinegar
1/4 cup California dry white wine
1/4 cup minced celery
1/4 cup minced scallions
1 can pineapple chunks (15-1/2 ounces), drained

Mix arrowroot or cornstarch with drained pineapple juice until smooth. Add soy sauce, white vinegar and wine and cook over low heat until sauce thickens, stirring constantly. Add celery and scallions and simmer for a few minutes, continuing to stir. Add pineapple chunks and simmer over very low heat for about 5 minutes. Pour over cooked fish. Also delicious on meat and chicken. Makes 1-1/2 cups.

III. PAPRIKA SAUCE

Spice up grilled or poached fish.

1 shallot or green onion, finely minced
1 large clove garlic, finely minced
2 tablespoons butter
2 tablespoons flour
1 cup bottled clam juice or fish stock
1/4 cup California dry white wine
1 tablespoon sour cream
1 tablespoon lemon juice
2 teaspoons paprika

Sauté minced shallot or green onion and garlic in butter until tender. Stir in flour and cook over low heat for 2 minutes. Gradually add clam juice or fish stock and wine, stirring constantly until well blended and thickened. Add sour cream, lemon juice and paprika. Makes 1 cup.

First sales room of the winery. Note the "wholesale and retail liquor dealer".

Lumache

After the snails were picked from the garden, Caterina would wash them under the faucet and keep only the ones that could crawl off a slick surface.

DAY 1: For at least 2 weeks she kept the snails in a box and fed them only cornmeal, greens and fresh water.

DAY 15: She took away the greens for 48 hours, but continued to feed them cornmeal and fresh water.

DAY 17: For the next 48 hours she took away the cornmeal, but left fresh water for them to drink.

DAY 19: When their systems were flushed out from this diet, she dropped the snails into a pot of boiling water and cooked them for 10 minutes. Then she removed them from the hot water, let them cool, and removed the meat from the shells.

The cooked snails were either fixed cioppino-style in tomato sauce or dipped in Joe Sciabica's Garlic Sauce or lemon juice.

Cod Navarro Style

Bacalao Navarro

Joe Larrañaga, a Delicato employee for 25 years, is currently sales representative in the Stockton and Manteca areas. Joe grew up in a home filled with the rich smells of Basque cooking since his parents came from the Spanish Basque provinces bordering France. Today, Joe and his wife, Theresa, cook traditional family Basque recipes and recipes gathered during a recent visit to the ancestral land.

2 pounds salt cod
2 medium onions, chopped
2 cloves garlic, minced
1 can minced pimientos (4 ounces)
1/4 cup olive oil
1 can tomato sauce (8 ounces)
1/2 cup minced parsley
1/2 cup Delicato Chablis Blanc

Wash the cod, changing water 3 or 4 times. Soak it overnight in water to cover. Drain. Cut fish into 2-inch pieces and place in cold water to cover. Bring to a boil and drain well.

Chop onions and garlic and fry with drained pimientos in olive oil. When vegetables are tender, stir in tomato sauce, parsley and wine. Cover and simmer for 30 minutes or until fish flakes easily. Serves 4 to 6 as an appetizer or main course.

Wine Suggestion: California Sauvignon blanc.

Joe's Garlic Sauce

1 head garlic, peeled (8 to 10 cloves)
1/2 teaspoon salt
4 to 5 sprigs parsley or sweet basil
1 teaspoon olive oil
1/2 to 3/4 cup cold water

Smash garlic in mortar, or grind lightly in blender or food processor. Add salt, parsley or basil, and olive oil. Mix well. Add water for desired consistency.

Poultry

Chicken Cacciatori

This family recipe is often served over rice or spaghetti.

1 chicken (3 to 4 pounds), cut up
4 tablespoons olive oil
Salt and pepper to taste
1 tablespoon dried, minced garlic
2 tablespoons minced parsley
2 teaspoons Italian Seasoning
1/2 cup thinly sliced mushrooms
4 cans tomato sauce (8 ounces each)
1 cup water
1 cup Delicato Rosé of Cabernet

Brown chicken pieces in oil until golden brown. Season with salt and pepper as chicken browns. Add garlic, parsley, Italian Seasoning, mushrooms, tomato sauce, water and wine. Cover and simmer for 35 minutes. Remove cover and simmer an additional 10 minutes. Serves 4 to 5.

Wine Suggestion: California Zinfandel.

Chicken In Chablis Wine

4 large cloves fresh garlic, peeled
3 tablespoons butter
3 tablespoons olive oil
1 chicken (3 pounds), cut up
Salt and pepper to taste
2 cups California chablis
1 can whole peeled tomatoes (28 ounces), cut into quarters

Sauté garlic in butter and oil in large pan. Brown chicken. Season with salt and pepper. Simmer until tender. Remove from pan and keep warm. Scrape bits of chicken off pan while stirring in wine. Reduce sauce by half over high heat. Add tomatoes, stir well and cook over moderate heat for about 10 minutes. Return chicken to pan, spooning sauce over chicken. Heat through and serve chicken in sauce. Serves 4.

Wine Suggestion: California chablis.

Classic Chicken In Wine

This recipe uses the traditional "Coq au Vin Bourguignon" ingredients and basic preparation procedures to produce a timeless success.

1/4 pound diced bacon
1 tablespoon butter
1 chicken (3 pounds), cut up
3 tablespoons brandy, warmed
1 yellow onion, chopped
1 tablespoon flour
2 tablespoons tomato paste
3 cups California Cabernet Sauvignon
2 large garlic cloves
1 large bay leaf
2 tablespoons minced parsley
1/4 teaspoon thyme
Salt and pepper to taste
1/2 pound fresh mushrooms
1 tablespoon butter

Sauté bacon in butter. Drain and reserve. Sauté chicken until nicely browned. Pour in warmed brandy. Ignite, shaking pan until flames subside. Remove chicken and keep warm.

In the same pan, sauté onion until translucent. Stir in flour and cook for 1 minute. Blend in tomato paste, wine, garlic and herbs. Season with salt and pepper. Bring to a boil, then lower heat and add chicken and bacon. Simmer for 1 hour, occasionally turning pieces in sauce. When chicken is done, remove to warmed platter. Increase heat and reduce sauce to about 3 cups.

Sauté mushrooms in 1 tablespoon butter until limp. Set aside. Return chicken to sauce and add mushrooms. Heat through. Serves 4.

Wine Suggestion: California Cabernet Sauvignon or Zinfandel.

Variation: Sauté 10 to 12 small white onions in 1 tablespoon oil and 1 tablespoon butter for 10 minutes. Braise in 1/2 cup white wine for 45 minutes. Add to chicken when adding mushrooms.

COQ AU VIN—PERFECT HARMONIZING OF CHICKEN AND WINE

Coq au Vin (coke oh van) is a French country dish in which the wine is every bit as important as the chicken. Together they simmer with onions and herbs, then are joined by mushrooms at the finish to create a hearty main dish.

Chanturge in France's Auvergne region claims it was the first to cook Coq au Vin, although the Burgundy area says it invented the popular dish. Today every province of France creates its own version, using wine from the area.

The traditional recipes used robust red wines, but soon white wines—even champagnes—became part of the recipe. Today, Coq au Vin recipes include almost every red and white wine. Julia Child urges her readers to experiment with different wines, renaming the dish "Coq au Riesling" or "Coq au Whatever," after the wine used. The *Joy of Cooking,* a popular cookbook, recommends a variation using sherry.

Delicato Vineyards suggest using Delicato red wines—Burgundy, Cabernet Sauvignon, or Barberone, and Delicato white wines—Chablis Blanc, Chardonnay, or Sauvignon Blanc. Try a different wine each time you prepare these recipes. You'll notice slight differences and will soon discover your favorite combination.

Mustard Chicken

In Sicily, Dad's grandfather and father made wine once a year from grapes they grew on a small plot of land near the house. When Dad came to this country, he did the same thing.

When Dad opened his winery, he no longer needed to make family wine, but he remembered others who did and provided them with bulk grape juice. Today, we still supply amateur winemakers with high-quality juice.

Each autumn during the crush, our parking lot is jammed with pickups and trailers loaded with empty wine barrels. Many of these home wine producers drive hundreds of miles, from as far away as Idaho and Arizona. Some come every year, getting here at 3 a.m. to claim a place in line. They visit with old friends, share winemaking secrets, and enjoy a picnic breakfast while they wait for the winery to open at 9 a.m.

It's not just the idea of saving money that brings people here. It's the excitement of being in touch with the land, the same excitement that comes from planting a garden or preparing a good meal. People like being part of a tradition that goes back to the founding of our winery and like recalling the customs of the Old Country.

Want to make a name for yourself? Fix this for your friends.

2 tablespoons butter
2 tablespoons olive oil
1 chicken (3-1/2 to 4 pounds), cut up
2 cups Delicato Chenin Blanc
1/4 teaspoon dried tarragon
Pinch thyme
1 large bay leaf
Salt and pepper to taste
2 egg yolks
2 tablespoons Country Style Dijon mustard (with seeds)
2 tablespoons sour cream
Pinch cayenne pepper

Melt butter in olive oil. Add chicken and cook until well browned. Add wine, tarragon, thyme, bay leaf, salt and pepper. Bring to boil. Cover and simmer 45 minutes. Remove chicken to heated serving dish and keep warm.

Discard bay leaf. Blend sauce with egg yolks. Add mustard, sour cream and cayenne. Heat, stirring continually. Do not allow to boil. Pour over chicken. Serves 4 to 6.

Serve with plenty of rice to soak up the wonderful sauce. Steamed carrots and zucchini slices are colorful and tasty additions. End with Peach Topping (page 129) over cinnamon ice cream.

Wine Suggestion: California Petite Sirah.

Roast Chicken

Boiling water
1 whole chicken (3 to 3-1/2 pounds)
1/2 lemon
2 garlic cloves, crushed
Paprika
Sesame Sauce (page 78)

Boil water. Preheat oven to 475°.

Rinse chicken in cold water and dry quickly. Rub skin and cavity of chicken with lemon half and garlic cloves. Place both in cavity. Put chicken in shallow roaster, breast side down. Sprinkle generously with paprika. Pour boiling water into roaster (but not on chicken) to a depth of one inch. Place on top rack of oven.

On lower rack, fill a shallow pan or pie plate with boiling water.

Roast chicken for 15 minutes at 475°. Turn chicken and lower heat to 350°. Cook for an additional 40 to 45 minutes. Keep at least 1/2 inch of water in roaster and ample water in lower pan. Serves 4.

Wine Suggestion: California Rosé of Cabernet.

Home winemaker. Grape juice buyer, 1982.

Rowdy Chicken

1 chicken (about 3 pounds), cut up
1 tablespoon dried rosemary
2 tablespoons olive oil
4 cloves garlic, minced
1/3 of 2-ounce can anchovies in oil
3/4 to 1 cup California dry white wine
3/4 cup heavy cream

Dredge chicken pieces in rosemary. Heat oil and sauté garlic until it begins to brown. Add chicken and fry until brown, turning often.

Mince anchovy fillets and mix with 1/2 cup wine. Pour over chicken and simmer uncovered 30 to 40 minutes. Baste occasionally with sauce, adding remaining wine.

Remove chicken to heated serving plate. To create sauce, add 3/4 cup heavy cream to skillet, stirring to loosen particles at bottom. Serves 4 to 6.

Add boiled new potatoes, a green salad and a lemony dessert and you'll feel transported to Greece.

Wine Suggestion: California Petite Sirah.

Chicken In White Port

Offers a touch of sweetness and a crunch of nuts.

1/2 cup golden raisins
1 cup Delicato White Port
1 chicken (3 pounds), cut up
1 tablespoon butter
1 tablespoon oil
1 medium onion, minced
6 whole cloves
1 bay leaf
1/2 teaspoon cumin
1 cup chicken stock
1/2 cup heavy cream
2 egg yolks
1/4 cup Delicato Green Hungarian
Salt and pepper to taste
1/2 cup (more if you wish) blanched, salted, whole almonds

Plump raisins in port. Brown chicken in butter and oil. Add onion, sautéeing until translucent. Add cloves, bay leaf, cumin and stock. Cover and simmer gently, adding port and raisins when chicken is half cooked.

When completely cooked, remove chicken to a heated serving platter and keep warm while preparing the sauce.

Mix cream, egg yolks and white wine. Stir in a small amount of hot chicken sauce and pour all into chicken pot. Stir gently for several minutes until slightly thickened. Do not allow sauce to boil. Serves 4.

Accompany with plenty of white or brown rice and steamed, chopped spinach.

Wine Suggestion: Delicato Green Hungarian or Rosé of Cabernet.

Sesame Sauce

1 cup Delicato Chenin Blanc
1/2 cup olive oil
1/4 teaspoon red pepper flakes (optional)
Salt to taste
2 garlic cloves, finely minced
1/3 cup sesame seeds, lightly toasted

Beat wine, oil, pepper flakes, salt and garlic together. Add sesame seeds. Serve over fish, chicken or meat. Makes about 2 cups.

Snohomish, Wash.
Oct. 20, 1938.

Jasper Indelicato,
Manteca, Cal.

Dear Sir:

We arrived home a week ago last Friday, after a very enjoyable trip through Cal., Nevada, and Utah. We enjoyed the wine we bought from you folks all the way home. The grapes were in fine shape when we arrived, and all of the family and friends had a taste.

We would like very much to have some more of your wine. Do you know if you can ship interstate? We could perhaps use a 5 gallon keg. If you have any information in regards to this would appreciate an answer from you soon.

Yours very truly,

O.H. Faulstich,
Snohomish, Wash.

P.S.: How did you like your horseradish root? Would you like some more?

Chicken With Nutmeg

Yes—a whole nutmeg is correct. Something mysterious happens as this sauce simmers.

1 chicken (3 pounds), cut up
3 tablespoons olive oil
2 medium onions, thinly sliced
3 large garlic cloves, minced
1 whole nutmeg, grated or 3 teaspoons ground nutmeg
1 teaspoon thyme
2 tablespoons minced parsley or cilantro
1 cup chicken broth, heated
2/3 cup California medium-dry sherry

Brown chicken pieces in olive oil in large pot. Remove chicken. Add onion and garlic to drippings and cook until soft and golden.

Mix nutmeg, salt, thyme and parsley (or cilantro). Add to onions, stirring well. Return chicken to pan. Add broth and half of sherry and bring to a boil. Reduce heat, cover, and simmer for 1 hour. Stir in remaining 1/3 cup sherry just before serving. Serves 4 to 5.

Accompany with brown rice, steamed carrots and a simple dessert of vanilla ice cream with a splash of Delicato Angelica.

Wine Suggestion: California burgundy.

Home winemakers at Delicato.

Crunchy Brown Rice

3 cups chicken stock
1-1/2 cups raw brown rice
1 teaspoon ground tumeric (optional)
1/3 cup dried currants
1/4 cup California dry sherry
2 tablespoons finely minced green onions
1/3 cup pine nuts (or sunflower kernels)
3/4 teaspoon minced preserved ginger
2 tablespoons butter

Boil stock and add rice. Bring to a second boil. Stir well, cover and lower heat until rice barely simmers. Cook rice until tender, about 45 minutes.

Remove from heat and stir in remaining ingredients. Let mixture absorb flavors a few minutes before serving. Makes 4 to 6 accompaniment servings. Especially delicious with ham and chicken.

Chicken In Feta Sauce

FACTS ABOUT FETA

Feta cheese (fet-ah) is commonplace in Greek and Balkan cooking. Soft, crumbly, and salty, this chalky white delicacy is made from ewe's or goat's milk and tastes a little like Roquefort. It is delicious on salads or vegetables. Spread it on unsalted crackers or buttered, crusty French bread for a quick, elegant hors d'oeuvre.

The sauce is so good you'll ladle it over mounds of white rice and spoon up every last bit.

3 tablespoons olive oil
1 chicken (3 pounds), cut up
1 tablespoon butter
3 medium yellow onions, thinly sliced
1-1/2 pounds peeled and chopped fresh tomatoes (or 28-ounce can)
1/2 cup California dry white wine
2 cloves garlic, minced
2 teaspoons dried rosemary
Freshly ground black pepper
Salt
1/2 pound Feta cheese, sliced paper thin

In a skillet heat 2 tablespoons olive oil. Halve chicken breast and brown 4 to 5 minutes on each side. Remove to platter. Sauté remaining chicken pieces for 15 minutes, turning occasionally. While chicken is browning, heat 1 tablespoon oil and 1 tablespoon butter in large skillet. Add sliced onions and cook over medium heat, stirring occasionally. Cook until translucent and slightly browned, about 15 minutes.

Add tomatoes (with juice if canned), wine, garlic and 1 teaspoon rosemary to onions. Season with black pepper. Withhold any additional salt until end of cooking due to saltiness of cheese. Add chicken pieces, covering well with onions and sauce. Cover and simmer over medium-low heat for 20 minutes.

Lay Feta cheese slices on top. Cover and cook 15 minutes. Additional wine or water may be needed during cooking. Taste and add salt, if needed. Ladle over ample helpings of white rice and sprinkle with additional pulverized rosemary when serving. Serves 4 to 6.

Wine Suggestion: Light-bodied Zinfandel.

Original winery. Note the tub used for washing bottles.

Chicken With Okra

Kota me Bamyes

An often neglected vegetable in many parts of the U.S.A., okra takes center stage in this light chicken dish. "Because it's low in calories, I can eat quantities of it when I diet!" George Panigiris, Delicato's District Sales Manager, said when he shared this recipe.

1 package frozen okra (10 ounces) or 1-1/2 pounds fresh okra
1/4 cup olive oil
1 chicken (about 3 pounds), cut up
1/2 cup olive oil
1 large onion, chopped (about 1 cup)
2 large cloves garlic, minced
1/2 cup Delicato Chenin Blanc

Steam frozen okra until soft. Place fresh or defrosted okra in small saucepan with 1/4 cup olive oil. Sauté over low heat until vegetable is lightly tinged with brown. Set aside. Or, place cut-up okra in 1/4 cup olive oil and bake in 250° oven for 1 hour. Stir occasionally to ensure even browning.

Brown cut-up chicken in 1/2 cup olive oil. Reduce heat, add onion and garlic and cook until limp. Add wine. Simmer for 1 to 2 minutes. Add okra, reduce heat and continue simmering for 30 to 40 minutes. Check chicken occasionally and stir lightly. Add more wine near end of cooking if needed to create enough sauce for spooning over chicken and rice. Serves 6.

A Greek salad and Coconut Cookies complete this Greek-inspired menu.

Wine Suggestion: California White Cabernet.

Okra Hint: To dissolve the gelatinous substance in okra, Greek cooks always soak the vegetable in vinegar before cooking. To prepare fresh okra, first wash vegetable and cut off stems. Place okra in bowl, adding 1/2 cup white or cider vinegar per pound of okra. Let stand 1 hour. Rinse thoroughly with cold water and drain. Proceed with recipe.

To prepare frozen okra, drop into boiling water. When pieces separate, drain well and place in bowl. Add 1/2 cup vinegar per pound of okra and let stand 15 minutes. Rinse thoroughly with hot water and drain.

Second home of two families. First house was burned by children playing with matches.

Chicken In Burgundy

You'll need more time to prepare this variation but you won't regret it. The smooth mouth-watering sauce is a combination of port, brandy and California burgundy.

1 chicken (3 pounds), cut up
2 tablespoons butter
1/2 pound mushrooms
1 tablespoon butter
3 slices bacon, minced
Minced chicken giblets
8 to 12 small, whole onions
3 garlic cloves
3 tablespoons brandy
2 cups California burgundy
Salt and pepper to taste
1 tablespoon butter
1 tablespoon flour

MARINADE:

2 cups Delicato Port
3 sprigs parsley
12 peppercorns
Bay leaf
1/8 teaspoon thyme

Prepare marinade of port, parsley, peppercorns, bay leaf and thyme. Marinate chicken in glass bowl 24 to 48 hours in refrigerator, turning occasionally.

Remove chicken from marinade and dry with paper towel. Strain and reserve marinade. Sauté chicken pieces in 2 tablespoons butter. At same time in separate pan sauté mushrooms in 1 tablespoon butter until limp. Remove.

In same pan fry bacon with minced chicken giblets. When ready, remove to paper towel. Still using same pan, brown onions and cloves in remaining grease until lightly brown. Add onions, garlic, bacon and giblets to chicken.

Add warm brandy. Ignite, shaking pan until flames subside. Add burgundy plus 1 cup of reserved marinade. Cook 1 hour over moderate heat. Taste for seasoning.

Remove chicken to serving platter and keep warm. Reduce sauce to approximately 3 cups. Add mushrooms and heat through.

Combine 1 tablespoon butter and 1 tablespoon flour in a bowl. Knead thoroughly, then shape into tiny balls. Just before serving, drop a few at a time into the sauce, beating briskly, until all are absorbed. Over low heat, stir sauce constantly for 1 or 2 minutes. Do not boil. Simmer for an additional 5 minutes and pour over chicken.

Wine Suggestion: California burgundy.

Persian Chicken

Roasted chicken stuffed with bulgur, reminiscent of Mideastern flavors.

1 roasting chicken (about 3-1/2 to 4 pounds), whole
Lemon wedge
Garlic clove
3 tablespoons melted butter
1/2 cup minced white onion (or green onions with some tops)
1/2 cup bulgur (parched, crushed wheat, sometimes labeled pilaf)
1/2 teaspoon cinnamon
1 cup chicken broth
1/3 cup tomato sauce
1/4 cup finely chopped dried apricots
1/4 cup raisins
1/4 teaspoon salt
Dash black pepper
1 teaspoon lemon juice
3 tablespoons honey
3 tablespoons butter
2 tablespoons California medium-dry sherry
3 to 4 tablespoons sesame seeds
Parsley sprigs
Lemon slices
Orange slices

Rub skin and cavity of chicken with lemon wedge and garlic clove. In medium saucepan melt 3 tablespoons butter. Add onion, sautéeing about 5 minutes. Add bulgur and stir constantly for 5 minutes. Add cinnamon, broth, tomato sauce, apricots, raisins, salt and pepper and lemon juice. Remove from heat. Let sit, covered, for 1 hour.

Preheat oven to 350°. In small saucepan heat honey, 3 tablespoons butter and sherry over low heat until butter melts. Stuff chicken with bulgur mixture and place in roasting pan. Roast in 350° oven for 1 hour and 15 minutes, brushing bird frequently with honey-butter-sherry mixture.

After 1 hour of baking, baste chicken for final time with mixture and drippings from pan. Scatter sesame seeds over chicken. Watch carefully for 15 minutes to avoid over-browning. Remove from oven, let stand 5 minutes before serving.

Place bird on platter and surround with sprigs of parsley and lemon and orange slices. Carve at table, giving each guest a hearty helping of the steaming-hot dressing. Serves 4 to 6.

Wine Suggestion: Delicato Green Hungarian.

Chicken With Spices

First fried crisp, then simmered in wine and spices, this chicken dish has a smooth texture and a sweet East Indian taste.

1 chicken (3 pounds), cut up
1/4 cup flour
1/2 cup olive oil
2 garlic cloves, minced
1 small onion, minced
1/8 teaspoon cinnamon
1/8 teaspoon cloves
2 cups California dry white wine
Salt to taste

Dust chicken lightly with flour. Heat olive oil in heavy casserole. Fry chicken until very brown and crisp. Remove chicken and pour off all but 2 tablespoons of oil.

Add garlic, onion, cinnamon and cloves and cook until onion is soft. Add wine and simmer for 10 minutes. Replace chicken and simmer uncovered for about 15 minutes, until chicken is tender. Check for seasoning. Serves 4 to 5.

Delicious with wild rice, baked yams and perhaps a fruity dessert such as Apple Slices Baked In Red Wine (page 127).

Wine Suggestion: California Rosé of Cabernet.

Chicken On The Hot Side

The cook can control the hotness. Appetites will expand after the first bite, so prepare plenty. It's even better warmed up, if there's any left! The recipe doubles easily for entertaining, keeps well in the refrigerator and improves with reheating.

2 tablespoons olive oil
3 pounds chicken pieces
1/2 cup shallots (or mild onions), minced
2 cloves garlic, halved
1 can whole tomatoes (28 ounces)
1 cup California dry white wine
1/2 teaspoon salt
1/4 teaspoon black pepper
1/4 teaspoon crushed red pepper or Tabasco to taste
1/3 cup minced parsley

Heat oil in skillet. Brown chicken pieces until golden. Place in large ovenproof casserole.

In same skillet, sauté shallots and garlic for 3 minutes, adding more oil if necessary. Stir in tomatoes, wine, salt and pepper, red pepper and parsley. Simmer for 10 minutes and pour over chicken. Bake 1 hour at 350°. Serve over spinach fettucine or egg noodles. Accompany with salad greens and a cooling fruit dessert such as Zabaglione (page127) drizzled over fresh fruit. Serves 4 to 6.

Wine Suggestion: California Robust Zinfandel or Cabernet Sauvignon.

Our entire family still remembers the Sunday in 1964 when the first glass-lined tanks arrived from Texas at the Turner Station siding, just down the road from the winery. Until this time, all our wine was aged indoors in wooden tanks.

The six used tanks were unloaded from the railroad flat cars with a crane, hauled to the winery, a half mile away, and placed on concrete foundations.

We were all there, taking movies of the whole event. When the tanks were safely in place, we sat down for a big family meal and celebrated our new winemaking capacity— 403,000 gallons—three times what we had been able to produce the year before.

Building fermenters, 1953.

Italian Stuffed Turkey

"In America, turkey is traditionally served on Thanksgiving or Christmas, but our family had it on all special occasions, including Easter.

"Mom fixed it the way she learned in the old country. When she added the potatoes, carrots and onions to the juice near the end of the cooking, we knew it was almost time to eat.

"Although her daughters-in-law Dorothy and Mary have each changed the original slightly to fit their tastes, my sister Frances, or Francy as we call her, still prepares it the way she remembers Mom cooking it. We include all three recipes in the book for you. We have never served a single wine with the turkey dinner, but instead put out a selection of wines and let every one drink his favorite."

—Vincent Indelicato

SOUTH ITALIAN STUFFED TURKEY—DOROTHY'S RECIPE

29-pound turkey
Dressing
1 cup white wine
Garlic salt to taste
Pepper
Celery and onions, sliced
Potatoes, peeled and halved

DRESSING:

4 pounds ground beef
5 eggs
2 cups rice, steamed with salt, butter and parsley
1 large onion, coarsely chopped
Salt and pepper to taste
4 tablespoons dried minced garlic
1 cup fresh parsley
2 cups Delicato Zinfandel
1 cup grated Romano cheese

In large bowl combine beef, eggs, cooked steamed rice, onion, salt, pepper, garlic, parsley, red wine and cheese. Mix well. Stuff turkey with dressing. Sprinkle with garlic salt and pepper to taste. Pour white wine over bird.

Place turkey in covered roaster and put in unheated 500° oven for 20 minutes. Turn down heat to 400° and bake for 4 hours without removing the lid. Check turkey, opening lid away from you to avoid the steam which has generated during cooking.

Add celery, onions and potatoes and cook covered for an additional 30 minutes.

Wine Suggestion: California Chardonnay or White Cabernet.

SOUTH ITALIAN STUFFED TURKEY—FRANCES' RECIPE

20 to 24-pound turkey
3 pounds ground beef
1 onion, chopped
3/4 cup cooked rice, cooled
Garlic to taste, minced
1 teaspoon olive oil
Parsley to taste, minced
1 cup Romano cheese, grated
Salt and pepper to taste
1 egg

Mix ground beef, onion, rice, garlic, parsley, cheese, and egg. Mix well. Stuff turkey and close tightly with skewers or thread. Rub bird with olive oil, salt and pepper.

Put turkey into covered roaster and place in unheated oven. Turn heat to 550° for 15 minutes. Lower oven temperature to 450° for 1 hour. Reduce heat to 400° for an additional hour.

After 2 hours and 15 minutes, remove lid on roaster and baste bird with drippings. Add peeled and quartered potatoes, carrots and onions. Cook covered at 375° for about 45 minutes, or until vegetables are cooked.

Wine Suggestion: California Sauvignon Blanc or White Cabernet.

SOUTH ITALIAN STUFFED TURKEY—MARY'S RECIPE

20 to 22-pound turkey
Dressing
Olive oil
2 cups (or more) Delicato Chardonnay
Salt and pepper to taste
Carrots, potatoes, celery (optional)

DRESSING:

2 cups cooked white rice, cooled
1-1/2 pounds lean ground beef
3/4 cup grated Romano cheese
1 egg
1/4 cup olive oil
3/4 cup minced parsley
6 large garlic cloves, chopped
Salt and pepper to taste

Rinse and dry turkey. Stuff with dressing. Rub bird with olive oil. Pour wine over turkey. Season skin of turkey with salt and pepper.

Preheat oven to 500°. Place bird in oven for 20 minutes, tightly covering the pan. Reduce temperature to 375° and cook bird for an additional 3 to 3-1/2 hours. Carrots, potatoes, and celery pieces may be added during the last 30 minutes of cooking. More liquid, wine or water, might be needed during the cooking time.

Wine Suggestion: California White Zinfandel or White Cabernet.

CRANBERRY MOLD

This colorful gelatin mold is a traditional turkey accompaniment at the Indelicato family Thanksgiving gatherings.

*1 package strawberry gelatin
   (6 ounces)
1 can whole cranberry sauce
   (14 ounces)
3/4 cup chopped apples
1/2 cup chopped celery
1/3 cup chopped walnuts*

Prepare gelatin as directed on package. When mixture begins to thicken, fold in cranberry sauce, apples, celery, and nuts. Refrigerate until set. Serve on lettuce leaves.

"While everyone waits for the turkey to be done, I serve appetizers. They're modern, compared to the rest of the traditional meal, but very good with wine. And not filling, so you can do justice to the meal. Italian cooking is not new to me—my maiden name is Celsi. I speak Italian and learned cooking from my mother."

—Mary Indelicato

Rabbit Stew

Umido Di Coniglio

1 rabbit (3 to 4 pounds)
2 tablespoons salt
4 tablespoons olive oil
1-1/2 cups chopped onions
Salt and pepper
1 can whole tomatoes (28 ounces) with juice
4 medium potatoes, peeled and quartered
1 cup hot water
1/4 teaspoon crushed red pepper

Cut rabbit into serving pieces. Place in pot and cover with water. Add 2 tablespoons salt. Let stand for 2 hours, then rinse rabbit under cold tap water and dry thoroughly with paper towels.

Heat olive oil in large skillet. Sauté rabbit pieces and onion for 20 minutes. Add salt and pepper to taste and continue browning. Add tomatoes, cover and simmer 20 minutes.

Add potatoes and water. Continue simmering for about 30 minutes or until rabbit and potatoes are tender. Serves 4.

Wine Suggestion: California Sauvignon blanc.

"Sometimes we grilled rabbit outside in the yard. Dad dug a hole and built a wood fire in it. When the wood had burned down to coals, he put a homemade grill across.

"After salting and peppering the rabbit pieces, I'd put them on the grill and brush them with olive oil. Because the grill was near the garden, I grabbed a handful of mint leaves, crushed them slightly and used them as a brush. They gave a bit of mint flavor to the meat."
—Frances Indelicato Sciabica

"We ate a lot of rabbit. We had hutches behind the house, with hundreds of rabbits. Sometimes I shot wild rabbits and then Mom would use those and conserve the tame rabbits for days when there was no other food.

"She usually fried the rabbit with garlic and added potatoes. We ate so much rabbit in those days that today I don't want any."
—Tony Indelicato

Papa and Mama with four children.

Meats

Basic Beef Burgundy

3 pounds lean, 2-inch stew meat cubes
1/2 cup flour
1/2 teaspoon salt
1/8 teaspoon black pepper
2 tablespoons olive oil
3 tablespoons butter
1/4 cup brandy or Cognac
3 slices bacon, diced
2 cups diced onion
2 cloves garlic, minced
3/4 cup thinly sliced carrots
2 tablespoons minced parsley
1 bay leaf
1/2 teaspoon thyme
3 cups California burgundy
12 small pearl white onions
2 tablespoons butter
1 teaspoon sugar
24 firm white mushroom caps
1 tablespoon butter

Roll meat cubes in flour seasoned with salt and pepper. Heat olive oil and 3 tablespoons butter in skillet and brown meat on all sides. Remove meat to casserole. Warm brandy, ignite and pour over meat.

Sauté bacon in skillet. When partially cooked, add onions, garlic and carrots and cook until limp. Add to casserole with parsley, bay leaf, thyme and wine. Cover and cook in 325° oven for 3 hours. After 2-1/2 hours of cooking, add onions which have been sautéed in butter with sugar until lightly brown.

Sauté mushrooms in butter and add during last 5 minutes of cooking. Remove casserole from oven and serve immediately or cool, cover and refrigerate for reheating in a day or two. Serves 6 to 8.

Plenty of French bread, boiled new potatoes plus a green salad with tart vinaigrette dressing complete this hearty meal. Finish, if you can, with fresh fruit or a chilled lemon mousse.

Wine Suggestion: California burgundy or Cabernet Sauvignon.

Variation 1

Familiar *Bouef Bourguignon* flavor in a beef roast.

3 garlic cloves, slivered
3-pound piece lean, boneless beef (chuck or cross rib)
Salt and pepper to taste
1 slice bacon, halved
Pinch cinnamon
Pinch nutmeg
4 cloves
1 onion, quartered
Bouquet garni of bay leaf, parsley and celery
2 carrots, halved and cut in thin strips
1 tablespoon diced bacon
1/4 cup brandy
2-1/2 cups California burgundy

Insert garlic slivers into beef roast and rub with salt and pepper. Place bacon slice on bottom of casserole with beef on top. Add cinnamon, nutmeg, cloves, onion, *bouquet garni,* carrots, diced bacon, brandy and wine. Liquid should almost completely cover meat.

Cover casserole with double thickness of waxed paper. Cover with lid and cook in 350° oven for 1 hour. Reduce heat to 250° and cook at least 4 hours longer. Skim fat from top before serving. Serves 4 to 6.

Wine Suggestion: California burgundy.

Grandma and Grandpa (founder) with grandchildren, 1960.

Frances Indelicato Sciabica,
daughter of founder.

Variation 2

2 pounds 2-inch stew meat cubes
1/4 cup flour
2 tablespoons vegetable oil or bacon fat
1/4 cup water
1 cup Zinfandel
1/4 cup flour mixed to a paste with 1/4 cup cold water
1/2 teaspoon salt
3 bay leaves
20 small whole black peppercorns
1 lemon, thinly sliced

Roll meat cubes in flour and brown in hot bacon fat or oil. Transfer to casserole. Drain fat from skillet and add water, loosening browned bits. Add wine, flour-water mixture and salt. Bring to a boil, stirring constantly until thickened. Pour liquid mixture over meat in casserole, adding bay leaves and peppercorns. Cover and cook 3 hours in 325° oven. Add lemon slices during last half hour of cooking. Serves 6.

To cook in crock pot: Place in crock pot and cook on low for 8 to 10 hours. Add lemon slices during the last hour of cooking.

Wine Suggestion: California Zinfandel.

Variation 3

3 pounds rump (or chuck) roast, cut into 1-1/2 inch cubes
Salt and pepper to taste
1/4 teaspoon ground allspice
1/2 pound lean bacon, diced
1/4 cup fresh minced parsley
1 clove garlic, minced
1 tablespoon minced shallots (or green onions)
1/4 teaspoon *each* rosemary, thyme and mace
1 onion, stuck with 6 cloves
3 cups Cabernet Sauvignon

Season meat with salt, pepper and allspice. Reserve. In a bowl combine diced bacon, parsley, garlic, shallots and herbs. Mix well. In a casserole place a layer of meat, then a layer of chopped mixture. Add a second layer of meat and mixture and end with a third layer of meat. Place onion with cloves in center. Pour red wine over all.

Bring to a boil for 2 minutes, cover tightly and simmer on stove top over low heat for 3 hours. Skim off fat before serving. If serving later, let grease solidify and remove before reheating. Serves 6 to 8.

Wine Suggestion: California Cabernet Sauvignon.

Beef With Blue Cheese

This ground beef dish leaves behind the word "hamburger" with mustard, ketchup and onion and moves up into the steak family.

1 pound ground round beef steak
2 ounces ham, minced (several slices from the deli case)
Salt and pepper to taste
2 ounces Blue cheese
1/2 cup California burgundy
2 tablespoons butter
Parsley for garnish

Mix ground beef with ham. Add small amount of salt and pepper. Cut cheese into 4 squares. Mold meat around cheese, forming into flattened patties. Place in shallow dish. Cover patties with wine and let stand, covered, in refrigerator about 4 hours. Before cooking, place 1 tablespoon butter in casserole, add half marinade and patties. Fry to desired doneness.

Remove patties to heated plate. Add remaining butter and boil on top of stove. Pour over patties. Garnish with parsley and serve. Makes 4 patties.

Wine Suggestion: California Cabernet Sauvignon.

Mary's Pot Roast

Beef roast (5 to 6 pounds)
2 tablespoons olive oil
1 onion, sliced
5 to 6 garlic cloves
1 can whole tomatoes (16 ounces)
2 cans tomato sauce (8 ounces each)
1 cup California burgundy wine
2 teaspoons Italian Seasoning

Brown beef on both sides in olive oil in large, flat pan. Place onions and garlic on top. Combine tomatoes, tomato sauce, wine, and Italian Seasoning and pour around meat. Cover and simmer for 2 hours over low heat on stove top or bake in 325° oven. Check occasionally, adding water, if necessary.

Wine Suggestion: California burgundy.

BURGUNDY VALENCIA

1 part orange juice
2 parts California burgundy
Fresh fruit
Ice cubes

Combine orange juice and wine. Stir. Add ice cubes, garnish with fruit and serve. For variety, add a sprig of fresh mint and a pinch of powdered sugar. Makes a single serving.

Begin a simple summertime lunch of minestrone, bread and cheeses with this refreshing drink.

93

Beef And Onion Stew

This onion-beef stew freezes well and warms up beautifully, making it a winner in the prepare-ahead department.

1/2 cup butter
3 pounds lean beef, cut in 1-1/2 inch cubes
Salt and pepper to taste
2-1/2 pounds small onions, peeled (about 32)*
1 bay leaf
1 small cinnamon stick
4 whole cloves
1/4 teaspoon ground cumin
2 tablespoons currants or raisins
1 can tomato paste (6 ounces)
1/3 cup Zinfandel
2 tablespoons red wine vinegar
1 tablespoon brown sugar
1 clove garlic, minced or mashed

Melt butter in heavy pot with cover. Season meat with salt and pepper and sauté briefly in butter. Do not brown. Arrange onions over meat.

Add bay leaf, cinnamon, cloves, cumin and currants. Combine tomato paste, wine, vinegar, sugar and garlic and pour over meat and onions. Place a plate on top of mixture to keep onions in place. Cover and simmer 3 hours, or until meat is very tender. Do not stir during cooking. As you serve, stir sauce gently to blend. Makes 6 servings.

Include a garlicky salad, crusty bread and Spanish Basque Flan.

Wine Suggestion: California Petite Sirah.

An equal amount of thinly sliced yellow onions may be substituted although the appearance and taste of the dish will be changed. Either way it's good.

Meatballs With Chorizo

Albondigas con Lukainka

Joe Larrañga tells how a quarter pound of spicy sausage transforms the ordinary meatball into a hot number. You'll love the red sauce.

1/4 pound chorizo sausage meat
1 pound lean ground meat
3/4 tablespoon salt
1 tablespoon minced parsley
1 can (8 ounces) tomato sauce
2 slices French bread with crust
1 egg, lightly beaten
1/4 cup flour (approximately)
4 tablespoons olive oil
1/2 cup Delicato Chenin Blanc
1 cup chicken stock or water

Squeeze chorizo meat from sausage casing into ground beef. Incorporate the clay-red chorizo with the brown-red beef to achieve an even color. Add salt, parsley and tomato sauce. Soak bread in small saucer of water for 2 to 3 minutes. Squeeze dry and add to meat mixture. Blend in beaten egg.

Divide mixture in half and begin forming meatballs. (You will get 10 to 11 "golf balls" from each portion of meat.) Place flour on plate or sheet of waxed paper. Roll meatballs in flour and place in hot oil in flat skillet. When balls are brown on one side, carefully turn over. Shake pan to prevent balls from sticking. Add wine and stock or water when balls are evenly brown. Cover and simmer for 30 minutes, shaking pan occasionally. Serves 4.

Joe suggests serving a green salad with a tart vinaigrette dressing. "Plenty of potatoes or rice are necessary," he adds, "to soak up the delicious sauce."

Wine Suggestion: California Robust Zinfandel.

Peppery Kebabs

Steak flavor with an added bite.

1-1/2 pounds, 1-inch boneless sirloin cubes
3/4 cup California burgundy
2 tablespoons olive oil
1/2 teaspoon salt
1/2 large, mild yellow onion, thinly sliced
1/2 teaspoon dried thyme
2 to 3 tablespoons peppercorns

Marinate meat cubes in glass bowl with wine, oil, salt, onion and thyme for 2 to 3 hours. Crack peppercorns with flat of knife blade and spread on flat surface. Thread steak cubes on skewers and roll lightly in pepper. Grill over very hot charcoal, turning once, about 3 minutes on each side for medium rare. Serves 4.

Wine Suggestion: California Robust Zinfandel.

Hint: If using wooden skewers for kebabs, soak in water for several hours or overnight to prevent excessive charring.

Steak Joan

1 to 1-1/4 pound sirloin steak, about 1 inch thick (individual
    4 ounce filet mignons make an elegant special occasion dinner)
1 tablespoon peppercorns, crushed
1 tablespoon butter
1 tablespoon olive oil
2 tablespoons California dry sherry
2 tablespoons heavy cream
1 tablespoon Dijon mustard

Crush peppercorns and pat into both sides of steak. Chill for several hours.

Melt butter and oil in heavy skillet.

Fry or grill steak over high heat until crisp on the outside but pink in the center. Remove to platter and keep warm while sauce is prepared.

Combine sherry, cream and mustard and add to skillet. Over low heat, stir mixture until hot. Pour over steak, garnish with parsley and serve immediately. Makes 4 moderate meat servings.

Wine Suggestion: California Zinfandel or Cabernet Sauvignon.

FESTA

Each summer, Portuguese-Americans in the Manteca area, like Dorothy Indelicato, observe a traditional festival that means good food, good times and most important—a chance to honor their common heritage.

The *Festa* (fesh-ta) commemorates the charity of Portugal's Queen Isabel, who asked the nobles of her kingdom to dedicate one day a year to the Holy Ghost. On this feast day, she proclaimed, they would give food and money to the poor.

After the parade and mass, which are part of the *Festa,* townspeople and Portuguese from surrounding communities enjoy a feast of traditional Portuguese foods: *Sopas,* sweet breads and *Tremocos,* lupine beans. Joe Teicheira, one of the renowned chefs of the local festival, shared his *Sopas* recipe, which feeds 640, with "Meet Delicato" readers:

Dorothy Cardoza.

Portuguese Sopas

Sopas

5-pound beef pot roast, cut into 3 pieces
4 cloves garlic
3 cans tomato sauce (8 ounces each)
1/2 cup coarsely chopped onion
1/2 cup chopped parsley
5 celery stalks, chopped
1 bottle Delicato Vin Rosé (750 ml)
10 cups cold water
1 teaspoon pepper
2 tablespoons salt
1 tablespoon ground allspice
1/2 teaspoon cumin seeds
4 bay leaves
1 tablespoon wine vinegar
1 head green cabbage, cored and quartered
1 loaf French bread, cut into 1-inch slices
25 whole fresh mint leaves, with stem—essential

Combine all ingredients except mint and bread in a large pot. Cover and simmer 6 hours. During last hour, uncover pot.

At serving time, cover bottom of large, shallow serving dish with bread slices. Lay lightly bruised mint leaves on top of bread so each piece is touched by mint flavor. Ladle hot *Sopas* on top and eat immediately with a hearty California Zinfandel, or one of Dorothy's favorite wines, Delicato White Zinfandel. Serves 6.

SOPAS FOR A CROWD

Pour 5 gallons cold water into a 100-gallon pot. Add cheesecloth spice bag containing: 4 large handfuls bay leaves, 3 large handfuls cinnamon sticks, 2 pounds slivered bell peppers, 3 pounds pickling spice, 2-1/2 pounds Italian Seasoning.

Add one 1200 pound cow (700 pounds dressed weight.) Fill pot with cold water to within 12 inches of rim (about 25 gallons). Add: 6 pounds salt, 5 gallons Delicato Vin Rosé, 24 pounds chopped onion, 1 pound dehydrated onion, 5 ounces vinegar, 1-1/2 pounds garlic, 1/4 pound *each* ground oregano, pepper, nutmeg, *ground* rosemary, allspice and cumin seed, 15 large heads cabbage (halved and cored), 4 gallons tomato paste, 3 gallons tomato ketchup, 5 ounces Worcestershire sauce.

Cover and simmer for 15 hours. When serving, place slices of day-old French bread and several whole mint leaves in large serving pan (two hundred loaves of bread and 400 sprigs of fresh mint are needed). Ladle hot *Sopas* on top.

Portuguese-American with spice-bag for Sopas.

Lamb Chops

Simple to prepare, yet elegant beyond compare. Very pretty, too.

4 lamb chops (about 5 ounces each)
1/2 cup Zinfandel, Cabernet Sauvignon or rosé wine jelly
 (red currant jelly may be substituted)
6 tablespoons California medium-dry sherry
4 orange strips*
Orange wedges

Broil chops, turning once, until crisp on outside, but still pink in center.
 Combine jelly, sherry and orange strips. Cook until hot and jelly dissolves. Place chops on heated serving platter and spoon sauce over chops. Garnish with orange wedges. Serves 4.

Wine Suggestion: California Green Hungarian.

Using knife or peeler, cut a 1/2-inch strip of orange peel from top to bottom of orange. Avoid cutting into white membrane, which is bitter.

First sales room of the winery.

Wine Jelly

Make a batch of wine jellies for gifts. Present them in small jars or wine glasses. You may use this recipe for other wines as well.

2 cups Zinfandel
3 cups sugar
3-ounce pouch liquid fruit pectin (1/2 cup)

Combine wine and sugar in saucepan. Bring to a boil. Add pectin and boil hard for 1 minute, stirring continually. Remove pan from fire, skim off foam and pour jelly into sterilized, warm glasses, leaving a 1/2-inch space at top. Seal with paraffin.

Shish Kebabs

The red wine marinade makes a difference. Use it for other lamb dishes as well.

2 pounds lamb cut into 1-inch cubes
16 medium whole mushrooms
1 large green pepper, cut into 1-inch chunks
2 medium onions, peeled and quartered
2 medium tomatoes, quartered

MARINADE:

1/4 cup olive oil
3/4 cup California dry red wine
1 onion, chopped
1 clove garlic, chopped
1/4 teaspoon basil
1/4 teaspoon marjoram
1/4 teaspoon rosemary
1 teaspoon salt
1/8 teaspoon pepper

Place lamb cubes in marinade for at least 8 hours, preferably overnight.

To cook, place lamb on skewers and grill 15 to 20 minutes, turning occasionally and basting twice with marinade.

Wipe mushrooms with damp cloth and parboil green pepper pieces for added tenderness, if desired. Arrange vegetables on 4 *separate skewers* and grill for the last 10 minutes, turning often and basting frequently with marinade. Serves 4.

Wine Suggestion: California White Zinfandel.

CORN BAKED IN FOIL

Corn is ready when it turns a vivid yellow. Serve with Shish Kebabs.

1 cob of corn, husked
1/2 teaspoon zippy horseradish
1/2 teaspoon Dijon mustard
Dash of salt
Dash of white pepper

Mix all ingredients and smear on corn. Wrap loosely in foil. Bake for 30 minutes in 450° oven or on grill. If grilling, check occasionally to avoid scorching. Add dash of water if completely dry.

Lamb With Orange

DELICATO

CALIFORNIA
SAUVIGNON BLANC
1984

PRODUCED AND BOTTLED BY DELICATO VINEYARDS
MANTECA, CALIFORNIA, U.S.A. BW 4094
ALCOHOL 12.0% BY VOLUME

Assertive flavors of lamb, thyme and garlic meld beautifully with orange in a country-style casserole.

1-1/2 pounds 2-inch boneless lamb cubes
Salt and pepper to taste
2 teaspoons powdered thyme
2 tablespoons olive oil
1-1/2 cups California dry white wine
2 tablespoons olive oil
2-1/2 cups thinly sliced white onions
2 cups peeled potatoes, cut into 1/2-inch slices
1 tablespoon slivered garlic, lightly bruised
4 1-inch wide strips of fresh orange rind
2 bay leaves
1/2 cup small black olives (Greek Calamata are best)
4 tablespoons finely minced parsley for garnish

Sprinkle lamb cubes with salt, pepper and thyme. Heat 2 tablespoons olive oil in heavy pan. Add lamb and sauté until browned. Remove meat to bowl. Add wine to pan, scraping up brownings on bottom of pan, and pour into bowl with lamb.

Heat 2 more tablespoons olive oil in same pan. Add onions, potatoes, garlic and orange rind. Cook for 5 minutes. Add bay leaves, lamb and wine. Simmer over very low heat for 1 hour or until potatoes are done, but not mushy.

Check seasonings. Remove bay leaves and orange rind. Add olives during last 5 minutes of cooking. Garnish with parsley. Serves 6.

Begin the meal with a Brie Pinwheel (page 30) and finish with a Chocolate Mousse (page 138).

Wine Suggestion: California Sauvignon blanc.

Leg Of Lamb

1 leg of lamb (about 4 to 5 pounds)
2 cups California chablis
1 onion, sliced
2 garlic cloves, halved
2 bay leaves
Salt
Freshly ground black pepper
4 bacon strips

Make a marinade of wine, onion, garlic and bay leaves. Marinate lamb at room temperature for several hours. Drain lamb, reserving marinade.

Sprinkle salt and black pepper on lamb and rub into meat. Place bacon strips over lamb and roast uncovered in 325° oven 30 to 35 minutes per pound, basting with reserved marinade.

Wine Suggestion: California Cabernet Sauvignon.

Corn Baked In Foil

Corn is ready when it turns a vivid yellow. Try it with some of the homemade mustard on page 109.

1 cob of corn, husked
1/2 teaspoon zippy horseradish
1/2 teaspoon Dijon mustard
Dash of salt
Dash of white pepper

Mix all ingredients and smear on corn. Wrap loosely in foil. Bake for 30 minutes in 450° oven or on grill. If grilling, check occasionally to avoid scorching. Add dash of water if completely dry.

Veal With Brandy Cream

Bill Nakata, Vice President in charge of Plant Operations, and his wife Karen often fix these two elegant recipes when they entertain.

4 slices veal (about 6 ounces each)
Flour for dusting
2 tablespoons butter (clarified preferred)
2 tablespoons olive oil
2 tablespoons butter (clarified preferred)
2 tablespoons chopped shallots
1-1/4 cups beef broth
1/4 cup brandy
3/4 cup thinly sliced fresh mushrooms
1/2 cup heavy cream
1 teaspoon arrowroot
2 tablespoons water

Gently pound veal between waxed paper. Lightly dust in flour. Heat oil and butter over medium heat. Sauté veal 3 minutes on one side and 2 minutes on the other. Place on warm platter.

Wipe skillet dry with paper towel. Melt 2 tablespoons butter and sauté shallots approximately 1 minute. Add beef broth and boil for 4 minutes. Add brandy and mushrooms and boil an additional minute.

Dissolve arrowroot in water. Add mixture with cream to pan. Stir continously until sauce thickens. Place veal slices in sauce and heat to serve. Makes 4 portions.

Wine Suggestion: California Chenin blanc.

Veal With Champagne

4 thin, boneless veal slices (about 6 ounces each)
Flour for dusting
2 tablespoons olive oil
2 tablespoons butter (clarified preferred)
4 thin, unpeeled lemon slices (rounds)
1 avocado, peeled, sliced thinly lengthwise
2 tablespoons butter (clarified preferred)
2 tablespoons chopped shallots
1/4 cup lemon juice
3/4 cup Delicato Champagne

Gently pound veal between wax paper. Lightly dust with flour. Sauté veal in butter and olive oil over medium to high heat for 3 minutes on one side and 2 minutes of the other. Place on warm platter.

Place lemon rounds on veal. Lay 4 to 5 avocado slices in fan design over each lemon round. Keep warm. Wipe out pan with paper towel and melt 2 tablespoons butter over medium heat. Quickly sauté shallots. Add lemon juice and champagne and boil for 1 minute, stirring continually. Pour sauce over veal and serve immediately.

This elegant entrée goes together just minutes before serving. Surround the golden veal with new potatoes boiled in their jackets, buttered asparagus, and salad greens.

Wine Suggestion: Delicato Chardonnay.

Osso Buco

As we married and had families, we all worked around the winery, especially during the busy crush time.

The children helped, too. Robert remembers standing on a box when he was only six years old to check empty bottles on the bottling line. A year later he drove a fork lift, even though he could barely reach the clutch. Joe Sciabica, Jr. recalls driving a tractor to dump stems and pumice in the fields when he was only seven. His sister Kathy helped in the bottling room, putting on seals.

By 1975, all Gaspare's grandchildren had jobs at the winery. Michael worked as a stockboy in the tasting room, Frank, Jay and Chris were in maintenance, and Cheryl and Marie worked in the office.

Now, Robert, after completing an enology degree, is Assistant Sales Manager, and Frank, Jr., after studying viticulture is supervisor of Farm Management. They are the third generation of Indelicatos to work in the family winery.

Ask your butcher for veal shanks if you don't see them in the case. An interesting variation in meal planning.

4 veal shin bones, 1-1/2 inch thick, weighing about 9 to 10 ounces each
1/4 cup flour
Salt and pepper to taste
2 tablespoons olive oil
2 tablespoons butter
1/2 cup minced carrot
1/2 cup minced onion
1/2 cup minced celery
1 bay leaf
1/2 teaspoon thyme
1 piece lemon peel (1/2 x 3 inches)
1 tomato, skinned, diced and seeded, about 1/2 cup (1 tablespoon tomato paste may be substituted)
1/2 cup beef broth
1 cup California dry white wine
Gremolata

Dredge bones in flour seasoned with salt and pepper. Melt oil and butter and brown meat evenly. Remove to platter.

In same pan, sauté carrot, onion and celery until soft. Add bay leaf, thyme, lemon peel and tomato. Return meat to pan.

Add broth and wine and pour over meat. Bring to a boil. Reduce heat and simmer covered to 1-1/2 hours, or until meat loosens and almost falls from bones. Remove bay leaf and lemon peel. Before serving, sprinkle with *gremolata* and simmer 5 minutes to meld flavors. Serves 4.

GREMOLATA:

1/3 cup minced parsley
2 cloves garlic, finely minced
2 teaspoons lemon rind

Combine freshly prepared ingredients and stir into hot veal dish. You may wish to adjust quantities to your taste preference.

Although traditionally served with a *risotto alla milanese,* steamed rice is quicker and soaks up the delicious sauce just as well.

When serving a crowd, present an Antipasto Tray (page 28) with wine before guests are seated at the table. A side dish of steamed spinach is all that is needed with the meal. Finish in Italian style with Anise Cookies (page 140) and coffee.

Wine Suggestion: California Sauvignon blanc.

Pork

Family Sausages

"Every winter we made sausage. We children cried during the slaughtering because we had raised the pig and became fond of the animal. But it was a busy day and soon we'd be in the middle of the sausage-making excitement and forget our sadness.

"Mom knew a lot about pigs from growing up in Italy. Her blood sausage made with pine nuts, Cream of Wheat and orange peel was a favorite. It tasted a little like mincemeat.

"She also rolled up hot chili pepper and fennel in strips of pig skin, tied them with string, and air-cured them. Later, she would boil and slice the "hot pork" for snacks or lunch.

"Today we still make the sausage from the same recipe, only now we get the ground pork from a butcher. When we were children, the sausages were cured and then packed in pork lard in gallon olive oil cans to preserve them. We never had a refrigerator, or even an ice box. Today, we cure the sausages for a few days and then freeze them.

"When the folks were first married, Dad heard that beef could be added to the traditional all-pork sausage. Even though Mom protested, he tried the combination. They buried a lot of sausage that year, she said, loving to tell the story. After that, they stuck to the original recipe.

"When we were growing up, these sausages were a mainstay of our diet. We'd come home hungry from school and barbecue a few on the ashes in the pot-bellied wood stove. Sometimes we'd throw whole garlic heads onto the coals and let them cook until they softened. Then we'd squirt them hot onto bread slices to eat them with the sizzling sausage.

"Now, once a year, usually the second Saturday of January, the family gathers in the basement of the old homestead to make sausage.

"The ground pork, about 300 pounds, is heaped onto an oil cloth covered table. The men measure out the chili peppers, salt and anise seeds and take turns blending the ingredients with their hands.

Sausage Party, 1985. Putting casings on machine. Vincent Indelicato and Dolores Cardoza.

"Joe and Mary Cardoza start washing the natural casings with water and lemons early in the afternoon. About six o'clock, the family starts to arrive, carrying food for a potluck supper. Wine is set out and a sample of the sausage meat is sautéed.

"Tasting the spicy sausage meat is the high point of the evening. There are always exaggerated gestures of pain, and good-natured arguments about whether it is hot enough.

"Dad used to say he had to make the sausage spicy or we kids would eat up a year's supply in a week. After we've filled up on the spiced meat, beans, salads, casseroles, bread and wine, we get to work.

"The men handle the sausage stuffer. As sausages come off the machine, one of the women ties the links and tosses them to the group waiting at the tables, where each link is pierced thoroughly with a fork. The children especially like this task.

"Frank supervises the hanging of the sausages. At one end of the basement, he carefully covers boards with white paper, then hangs the completed sausages up to cure.

"There's plenty of time to talk as we are together for five to six hours. The little ones get tired and sometimes curl up to sleep. The older children often bring their dates. Maybe it's a good way to see if they'll fit into the family.

"After the sausages are made, the desserts are uncovered and served with coffee. It's nearly midnight when the last person leaves and the light is turned off. A few days later everyone will return to the house and claim a share of the sausage."

—The Indelicato Family

Sausage Party, 1985.

Family Sausages

Makes Enough For The Whole Family!

Dorothy warns, "For the fainthearted, use half as much chili pepper. We like it hot!"

1 package (hank) casings
Orange or lemon slices from 3 oranges or lemons
100 pounds coarsely ground pork butt (35 percent fat)
2.9117 ounces crushed chili pepper
2 pounds salt
3 pounds mild California chili pods
3 cups anise seeds
String
Plus at least 2 dozen helping hands!

Freshen casings by washing in cold water with orange or lemon slices.
    Let casings soak while preparing meat.
    Remove stems from chili pods and grind coarsely. Mix meat with crushed chili peppers, salt, ground chili pods and anise seed. Test sausage for seasoning by frying some in a skillet. At this point, you may shape some sausage into individual breakfast patties separated with paper, and freeze.
    Fill casings with meat. Tie off at desired length. We make our links about 36 inches long.* Pierce sausages all over with fork. Hang in a cool place for 24 hours.
    This is fresh sausage, made with uncooked meat and not smoked or cured after filling. It must be frozen immediately after the hanging time, or refrigerated and eaten within 3 days. Makes approximately 65, 36-inch links.

*Cut to 3 inches when broiling.

Sausage Party, 1985.

Family Sausages

Just Enough For One Family

5 casings
8 pounds coarsely ground pork butt or pork loin
1 tablespoon crushed chili pepper
5 teaspoons salt
3 ounces mild California chili pods (coarsely ground*)
4 tablespoons anise seed
String

Follow the same directions for the larger recipe. Makes about 5, 36-inch links.

*The drier the peppers are, the easier they are to grind.

COOKING THE SAUSAGE

Each family member takes a share of the sausage home, and cooks it differently. All agree, however, that the sausage tastes best grilled over charcoal or oven broiled. Always prick the sausages before cooking to avoid bursting.

Alice Indelicato and Frances Indelicato Sciabica usually broil frozen sausages right from the freezer.

Mary Indelicato likes to defrost the sausages in the microwave oven, then broil them in the oven.

Dorothy Indelicato defrosts the sausages quickly in the microwave oven or slowly in the refrigerator. If she broils them frozen, halfway through cooking, she will cut the sausages lengthwise and lay them skin side down, so the inside gets thoroughly cooked.

RED WINE MUSTARD

Rosy in color, this zippy condiment is a pleasant surprise on ham or liverwurst.

1/4 cup mustard seeds
1/4 cup California red wine
1/3 cup red wine vinegar
1/4 cup water
1/2 teaspoon honey
1/4 teaspoon ground allspice
1/4 teaspoon black pepper
1 teaspoon finely minced garlic
1-1/2 teaspoons coarse kosher salt
1 bay leaf, finely crumbled

Combine the mustard seeds, wine and wine vinegar in a dish, and let stand for 3 hours. Do not extend time or seeds will absorb too much liquid.

Place water, honey, allspice, pepper, garlic, salt and bay leaf in blender and whirl to a coarse texture. Put mixture in top of double boiler. Stir over simmering water for 5 to 10 minutes, or until the mustard has thickened somewhat, but is not as thick as prepared mustard. Scrape mixture into a jar, let cool and refrigerate. Mustard will keep indefinitely. Makes 3/4 to 1 cup.

Sausage Party, 1985. Perforating casings. Chris Indelicato and Lori.

Ham Baked In Wine

A lovely pink ham surrounded by red accent.

1 ham (8-pound canned or precooked)
1/2 bottle Delicato White Zinfandel

Preheat oven to 350°. Place ham in rack in baking pan. Pour wine over ham. Roast according to directions, basting frequently. Let rest for at least 15 minutes before slicing. Delicious hot or cold. Garnish with spiced apples or Cranberry Apples .

Wine Suggestion: California White Zinfandel.

Cranberry Apples

Dress up your presentation with this tasty fruit garnish.

1 large baking apple per person (Rome Beauty, Golden Delicious,
   Jonathan, McIntosh)
Whole cranberry sauce
1/3 cup Delicato White Port per apple
Cinnamon

Core apples to within 1/2 inch from bottom. Carefully slice off bottom, allowing apples to stand upright in baking dish. Fill center with cranberry sauce.

Prepare as many apples as desired. Place next to one another on dish so apples remain upright. Pour port over apples and sprinkle liberally with cinnamon. Bake in 350° oven for about 30 minutes, basting with wine several times. Near end of baking time, test apples for doneness. Apples should be soft, but not mushy.

Let apples cool a few minutes, then slice in half through cranberry center. Place apple halves on serving platter, skin side down. Spoon baking liquid over apples and garnish platter with orange slices. Serve hot or cold.

Sausage Party, 1985. Preparing to fill sausage maker are Anthony Indelicato, Edward Cardoza, Michael Lavieri, Vincent Indelicato, Dorothy Indelicato, and Dolores Cardoza.

Pork Chops With Fennel

An easy sauce makes itself while these chops simmer. The fennel seeds add a pleasant, new taste.

2 tablespoons olive oil
3 to 4 cloves garlic
4 pork chops (1/2-inch thick)
Salt and pepper to taste
1/4 teaspoon (or more) fennel seeds
3/4 cup California dry red wine

Heat oil in skillet. Brown garlic and remove. Rub chops with salt, pepper and fennel seeds. Fry them on both sides until brown. Add red wine and cook uncovered until chops are tender. Spoon sauce over chops. Serves 2 or 4, depending on the weather and the hunger.

Accent the fennel flavor with a fresh *finocchio* and red radish salad. Creamed potatoes or baked potatoes are good wintertime additions. In summer, corn on the cob is colorful and easy.

Wine Suggestion: California Zinfandel or Chardonnay.

Sausage Party, 1985. Perforating sausage are Marie Indelicato (Dorothy's daughter), Mary Indelicato (Tony's wife), and Leslie Bloudoff (girlfriend of Robert).

Pork And Sage Supper

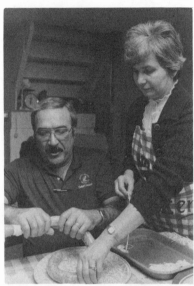

Sausage Party, 1985. Filling casings. Vincent and Dorothy Indelicato.

Sage is the dominant flavor. Small portions served with ample helpings of wild rice are satisfying.

3 pounds pork loin or shoulder
Freshly ground pepper to taste
4 tablespoons olive oil
2 medium onions, chopped
4 teaspoons sage
2 bay leaves
1/3 cup finely chopped parsley
1 teaspoon thyme
3/4 cup California dry white wine
1/2 cup hot water
1/2 cup white vermouth
1/3 cup capers

Trim fat and bones from meat and cut into 1-inch cubes. Sprinkle with pepper. Heat oil in large skillet and brown pork cubes on all sides.

Lower heat. Add onions, sage, bay leaves, parsley and thyme. Stir well. Add wine and hot water. Cover and simmer for 1 hour stirring occasionally and adding more white wine to keep liquid.

Remove meat to heated platter. Add vermouth to skillet and boil a few minutes, scraping up browned parts. Return meat to pan and add capers. Simmer to reheat. Serves 6.

Serve with wild rice, salad greens mixed with walnuts and orange slices and corn bread with lemon butter.

Wine Suggestion: California burgundy.

Sweet And Sour Pork

During berry season precede this meal with Strawberry Sangria and toasted almonds.

1 pound lean pork, cubed
Salt and pepper to taste
2 cloves garlic, slivered
2 tablespoons oil
1/2 cup water
1/2 cup Delicato Vin Rosé
1 can pineapple chunks (13-1/2 ounces)
1 cup pineapple juice reserved from can
1 tablespoon soy sauce
3 tablespoons wine vinegar
2 tablespoons cornstarch
3/4 cup coarsely chopped green pepper (1/2 x 1-inch pieces)

Season pork with salt and pepper. Brown pork with garlic in oil in skillet over medium heat. Reduce heat, and add water and wine. Cover and simmer 30 minutes. Mix pineapple juice, soy sauce, vinegar and cornstarch until smooth. Add to meat mixture and cook until sauce is clear and thick.

Stir in pineapple chunks and green pepper pieces. Cook uncovered for 5 minutes, stirring occasionally. Serve over steamed white rice. Serves 2 to 3 as a main dish, or 4 to 5 if part of an Oriental buffet.

Wine Suggestion: Delicato White Cabernet.

STRAWBERRY SANGRIA

1 cup thinly sliced strawberries
1/2 cup sugar
1 whole lemon, thinly sliced
1 bottle Delicato Zinfandel 750 ml
2 cups club soda

In large bowl combine strawberries, sugar and lemon slices. Stir mixture, bruising the fruit lightly. Pour in wine, cover and chill at least 1 hour. Remove lemon slices.

In punch bowl or large pitcher, blend wine mixture with club soda. Add ice to glasses. Ladle or pour wine into glasses. Serves 6.

Sausage Party, 1985. Filling casings.

Chops With Wild Rice

The greens of parsley and chervil plus the earthy flavors of pine nuts and wild rice make this naturally good.

2 slices bacon, or 2 tablespoons bacon drippings
4 pork chops
2 cups cooked wild rice
2 to 3 tablespoons finely minced green onions
4 tablespoons pine nuts (substitute pecans but not walnuts)
2 tablespoons minced parsley
1/2 cup Delicato Green Hungarian
2 to 3 tablespoons orange zest
1/2 teaspoon chervil

Cook wild rice until moist but not watery.

Fry bacon slices, reserving 2 tablespoons grease. Crumble bacon into small pieces and set aside. Fry pork chops in bacon drippings until crisp on both sides. Place in single layer in ovenproof casserole.

Combine hot rice with bacon pieces, onions, pine nuts, parsley, wine, orange zest and chervil. Mix well and spread over pork chops. Cover and bake 1 hour at 325°. Check occasionally, adding more wine if necessary. Serves 4.

Wine Suggestion: Delicato Green Hungarian.

Sausage Party, 1985. Frank Indelicato hanging sausages to cure.

Vegetables

Broccoli in White Wine

Go ahead and increase the garlic, if you like. The sauce is good on other vegetables, including boiled potatoes.

1 large bunch broccoli
1/2 cup California dry white wine
3 tablespoons olive oil
2 garlic cloves, slivered
2 tablespoons lemon juice
2 tablespoons minced parsley

Wash broccoli, removing leaves, trimming flowerettes, and cutting stems into 1/2-inch pieces. Steam stem pieces until almost tender (about 15 minutes). Add flowerettes to stems and steam until both are tender but not mushy (about 5 minutes).

In separate small saucepan, simmer wine, olive oil, garlic, lemon juice and parsley for 10 minutes. Place broccoli in heated serving bowl. Pour hot sauce over vegetable and toss lightly. Serve immediately. Makes 4 to 6 portions.

In the seventies we brothers formed a corporation and renamed the winery Delicato Vineyards. How we wish Dad and Mom could have been at the dedications of the new buildings in 1975 and 1983. They never imagined these buildings, especially the tower, would spring up where they once tended a big garden.

Cornmeal Potatoes

Turn plain potatoes into crusty, cornmeal-coated spuds. Very good with fish, roasted meats and poultry.

5 medium potatoes (about 1 pound)
1/2 cup cornmeal
1/4 teaspoon salt
1/4 teaspoon white pepper
3 tablespoons vegetable oil
3 tablespoons butter

Peel potatoes and halve through center. Cook until barely done. Drain, and set aside to cool enough to handle.

Melt oil and butter together. Use 1/2 teaspoon of mixture to lightly grease glass pie plate or shallow casserole large enough for potatoes to bake in single layer. Pour remaining mixture on small plate.

Combine cornmeal, salt and pepper on plate. Roll slightly warm potatoes first in oil/butter mixture and then in cornmeal mixture. Place in greased pie plate. When potatoes are all coated, drizzle some more butter/oil over them.

Bake uncovered in preheated 475° oven for 15 minutes. Drizzle remaining butter/oil over them during baking. At end of 15 minutes, broil for a minute to ensure a last-minute browning. Serves 3 to 4.

Sherried Asparagus

A combo of nuts, mustard, and cheese jazzes up asparagus spears. For a light wintertime supper, cut asparagus into chunks and ladle in sauce over split baked potatoes.

2 tablespoons butter
1/2 cup thickly sliced fresh mushrooms
2 tablespoons butter
2 tablespoons flour
1 cup half-and-half cream
Salt to taste
1/4 teaspoon dry mustard
3 tablespoons California dry sherry
1 pound asparagus spears, cooked *al dente*
1/2 cup toasted, slivered almonds
1/3 cup grated Parmesan (or your favorite) cheese

Over low heat, sauté mushrooms briefly in butter. Remove and add additional 2 tablespoons butter to same skillet. Gently stir in flour, making a roux. Cook at least 3 minutes, then slowly whisk in cream. Add salt, mustard and sherry. Cook until thickened.

Place asparagus in a shallow baking dish. Top with almonds and mushrooms. Pour sauce over all and sprinkle cheese on last. Place under broiler until cheese is melted and bubbly. Serves 4.

Accompany with crisp cole slaw and ham slices.

Wine Suggestion: California Rosé of Cabernet.

Herbed Cabbage

Spoon this creamy vegetable into a big baked potato, split and oozing with butter, for a light, meatless supper.

6 cups shredded cabbage, loosely packed
2 tablespoons butter
1/2 teaspoon salt
1/4 teaspoon white pepper
1 tablespoon pesto (see page 61)
1/2 cup California dry white wine

Cut cabbage into 1/2-inch strips. Melt butter in large skillet or wok. Add cabbage and toss until limp. Add salt, pepper, pesto and wine. Cover and simmer until tender, about 15 minutes. Just before serving, turn heat high for a few minutes to evaporate moisture. Serve hot. Serves 4 to 6.

PATIENCE MAKES A GOOD ROUX ...

A perfect sauce takes time at the start. You can assure a good roux by gently and continually stirring equal amounts of butter and flour over low heat for at least 3 minutes. Low heat prevents the flour from burning. Constant stirring distributes the heat, allowing the starch granules to swell evenly so they can absorb the liquid that you will add in the next step.

Delicato
Northern California
Cabernet Sauvignon

Produced and Bottled by Delicato Vineyards
Manteca, California.   Alcohol 12% by Volume.

Onions In Wine

A cool, refreshing relish to serve with ham. Also excellent with ham and rye sandwiches.

4 cups thinly sliced Bermuda onions
1 teaspoon salt
1/8 teaspoon white pepper
2 cups California dry white wine
Parsley sprigs for garnish

Place onions, salt and pepper in wine and chill for several hours or overnight. Garnish with parsley sprigs. Makes 4 cups.

Variation: For a brighter, rosier look, substitute red onions and Delicato Rosé of Cabernet and use plenty of freshly grated black pepper.

Eddie Cardoza, age 3, helping at 1985 Sausage Party.

Portuguese Beans

"We often serve these beans with steak, Italian sausage or barbecued mackerel," says Dorothy. "And the best wine is a red—Zinfandel or burgundy." Dorothy also says that fresh dried beans make a real difference.

1 pound pinto beans
6 cups water
2 tablespoons minced parsley
1/2 teaspoon pepper
1 medium onion, finely minced
1/2 teaspoon cumin
1 can tomato sauce (8 ounces)
4 slices bacon
1 tablespoon salt

Rinse beans and place in water. Add parsley, pepper, onion, cumin and tomato sauce. Stir. Bring to a boil and simmer 2 to 3 hours, or until beans are soft, but not mushy.

   Cut bacon into 1/2-inch pieces and fry until crisp. Add bacon and drippings to beans. Add salt to taste. Simmer for 30 minutes. Add more tomato sauce, if desired. Serves 6.

Red Pepper Gratin

Capture summer sunshine in this mild red pepper vegetable dish. An excellent accompaniment to grilled meat, especially lamb.

1 tablespoon olive oil
6 large ripe tomatoes, cut into 1/4-inch rounds
3 red bell peppers, chopped into 1/2-inch pieces
1 cup chopped parsley
2/3 cup fresh chopped basil
Freshly ground pepper (be generous)
1/2 cup California dry white wine
2 tablespoons capers, drained
1/2 cup unseasoned bread crumbs
4 tablespoons olive oil

Heat oven to 400°. Oil an enamel or glass casserole with 1 tablespoon oil. Cover the botton with 6 or 8 tomato rounds. Sprinkle with one third of chopped bell peppers. Combine parsley, basil and pepper. Add a layer of herb mixture on top of peppers.

Repeat 2 additional layers, ending with herbs. Pour wine over mixture. Combine capers and bread crumbs and spread on top. Drizzle olive oil over all. Bake uncovered for 20 minutes or until top is lightly brown. Delicious hot or chilled for several hours—even good cold the next day. Serves 4 to 6.

To a meat entrée, add rice, French bread and a lemony dessert.

Wine Suggestion: California Zinfandel.

Dad was a farmer. He didn't set out to be a winemaker. He borrowed money to buy 68 acres in 1923 so he could grow food for his family and earn his living farming. It was rolling land, mostly dairy fields. Bit by bit he leveled it and began to plant. His gardens were near the house. One of the gardens was exactly where our conference room is now. Sometimes on warm, sunny days when we sit inside and talk facts and figures, we all miss that earlier simplicity.

Dad's vegetable garden was the envy of everyone around here. He planted grapes, walnuts, almonds, figs, onions, garlic, cranberry beans, green beans, lettuce, carrots, peaches, apricots—even artichokes.

And lots of chicory, which he loved and grew till the day he died. He also planted prickly pears to remind him of Sicily. People who knew the pears from there would sometimes stop and ask Dad if they could have a few.

The Manteca area was like a Little Sicily for Dad. The warm weather, the sandy loam soil and the crops were like the Old Country. "You can leave Manteca and go to Sicily and hardly know you've left California," he said.

Children of founders, 1937.

Sweet And Sour Onions

Beautiful to look at, easy to make, and wonderful to eat with so many foods.

1 tablespoon olive oil
1 tablespoon butter
2 pounds peeled red onions, cut into 1/4-inch slices
2 whole cloves
3/4 cup California dry white wine
4 tablespoons red wine vinegar
2 teaspoons sugar
Salt to taste

Heat oil and butter in heavy skillet (not aluminum). Sauté onions and cloves until onions begin to brown and turn soft. Sprinkle with 1/2 cup wine, 2 tablespoons vinegar and sugar.

Reduce heat, cover and simmer for 20 minutes, stirring often. Add remaining 1/4 cup wine as needed. Transfer onions to heated serving platter. Add remaining 2 tablespoons vinegar to pan, boil a minute, and pour over onions. Serve at room temperature. Can be prepared the day before serving.

Cheesey French Loaf

Zippy surprise center in crusty bread loaf.

1 large loaf French bread, halved horizontally
8 to 10 thin slices mild Swiss cheese
1/3 cup California dry sherry
1/4 cup mayonnaise
1 can mild green chilies (4 ounces), drained

Lay French bread halves cut side up. On one half of bread, place thin slices of cheese. On other half, drizzle sherry. On top of this moistness, spread mayonnaise and sliced green chilies. Put halves together, forming whole loaf. Wrap in foil and bake in hot oven until cheese melts and crust is crisp. Slice vertically for hors d'oeuvres or cut into hearty chunks to serve as picnic fare or as a sandwich with bowls of soup.

Wine Suggestion: California Zinfandel or French Colombard.

Sherried Sweet Potatoes

Lightly sweet potatoes accented with orange zest.

6 medium sweet potatoes (about 3 pounds)
3 tablespoons butter
2 tablespoons grated orange rind
3/4 cup California medium-dry sherry
Butter to grease casserole
Cinnamon and nutmeg to taste

Cook potatoes until done but not mushy. Peel and slice into a bowl. Mash with mixer or food processor, adding butter and orange rind. Add sherry and stir well. Sprinkle with cinnamon and nutmeg. Bake covered at 350° for 30 minutes or until heated through. Serves 4 to 6.

Squash Cups

Acorn squash halves baked with sherry, nuts—or meat.

1/2 small acorn squash per serving
1 tablespoon brown sugar per serving
1 tablespoon curried walnut pieces per serving
1 tablespoon California cream sherry per serving
Butter

Cut acorn squash in half, removing seeds and shreds. Salt lightly and bake cutside down on cookie sheet in 350° oven until done but not mushy. Place halves upright in casserole. Sprinkle each with sugar, walnuts and sherry. Dot with butter and bake 10 additional minutes.

CURRIED WALNUTS:

Place broken walnut pieces on cookie sheet. Sprinkle lightly with olive oil, salt and curry powder. Bake in 150-200° oven until crunchy and pleasantly brown. Cool before adding to squash recipe.

Wine Suggestion: California Zinfandel.

Variation: For a one-dish meal, sauté ground beef with a touch of onion. Mix curried nuts, salt and pepper and fill center of squash. Bake until hot. Makes a single serving.

Vegetable Kebabs
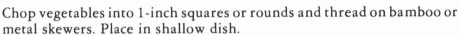

Grill alongside meat and poultry.

Assorted fresh vegetables: onions, green and red peppers, mushrooms,
    zucchini, eggplant, summer squash, etc.
1/2 cup olive oil
1/3 cup tarragon vinegar
1 tablespoon finely minced parsley
Salt and pepper to taste

Chop vegetables into 1-inch squares or rounds and thread on bamboo or
metal skewers. Place in shallow dish.

Mix olive oil, vinegar, parsley and salt and pepper. Pour over
kebabs and let marinate for at least 2 hours, turning kebabs once.

Grill in oven or over charcoal fire, brushing kebabs with marinade
and turning often. Remaining marinade may be heated with a dab of
butter. Use as a sauce to pour over cooked vegetables.

Variation: Beef or lamb cubes may be added to kebabs.

Red Cabbage

Simmered slowly in wine, this year-round vegetable accompanies
chicken and meat in a tasty way.

1 medium head red cabbage
4 slices bacon, chopped
2 medium tart apples, thinly sliced
1/4 teaspoon caraway seeds (optional)
1/4 cup cider vinegar
1/3 cup brown sugar (or 2 tablespoons honey)
Dash salt
1 cup California dry red wine

Remove tough outer leaves and hard core from cabbage. Cut or shred
cabbage coarsely. Soak in cold water for at least 15 minutes.

Fry bacon pieces in deep pan. Remove cabbage from water and
place in pan. Simmer for 10 minutes with bacon and grease, stirring
occasionally. Add apples and caraway seeds.

Combine vinegar, sugar or honey, salt and wine and pour over
cabbage. Cover and simmer for 1 hour and 15 minutes. Check
occasionally to make sure there is some liquid. If liquid remains after
cooking, uncover and simmer until it is absorbed. Makes 6 to 8 servings.

Zucchini Vinaigrette

Fix this crunchy condiment days ahead and keep cool.

2 tablespoons finely chopped green pepper
2 tablespoons finely chopped parsley
2 green onions, finely chopped
1 red pepper, finely chopped
1 clove garlic, crushed
3 tablespoons sweet pickle relish
1/2 cup salad oil
1/4 cup wine vinegar
1 teaspoon salt
2 teaspoons sugar
1/4 cup California dry white wine
6 long, slender zucchini

Combine all ingredients except zucchini, blending well. Cut ends from zucchini, but do not peel. Cut into lengthwise strips, about 6 strips to each zucchini. Cook in boiling salted water for about 3 minutes. Drain and arrange in bowl. Pour wine mixture over zucchini and marinate several hours. Serve with additional marinade.

Walnut Garlic Sauce

A delicious sauce that turns plain steamed vegetables—green beans, wax beans, potatoes—into a special dish.

2 egg yolks
2 tablespoons mild white wine vinegar
1 tablespoon lemon juice
3 garlic cloves
1/2 teaspoon salt
1 cup olive oil
1/2 cup ground walnuts

Place egg yolks, vinegar, lemon juice, garlic and salt in blender. Mix well. With blender on lowest speed, gradually add oil, blending until smooth. Stir in walnuts. Makes about 2 cups sauce.

Zippy Zucchini Spears

6 long, slender zucchini
2 tablespoons *each* finely chopped green pepper, red pepper and parsley
2 green onions, finely chopped
1 clove garlic, crushed
1/2 cup salad oil
1/4 cup wine vinegar
2 teaspoons sugar
1/4 cup California dry white wine

Trim ends from zucchini, but do not peel. Cut into lenghtwise strips, 4 strips to each half zucchini.

Steam for 2 to 3 minutes until *al dente*. Drain and place in shallow dish. Combine remaining ingredients and pour over zucchini. Marinate several hours. Serve as cold vegetable with marinade or drain, using zucchini spears as garnish. Reserve marinade for other vegetables.

Fruits

Cantaloupe In Port

Take along on a picnic—add nuts at the last minute.

1 summer melon except watermelon (or try a combination of melons)
Delicato White Port
Crushed pistachios

Cut melon in half and remove the juice, seeds and shreds. Scoop out flesh in bite-size balls and place in glass bowl. Pour wine over balls to cover. Chill. Serve fruit in dessert dishes with some wine. Sprinkle crushed pistachios on top *at last minute only.*

Poached Zinfandel Figs

Zinfandel is wonderful to use for poaching fruit. Try plums for a seasonal change.

1-1/2 cups Zinfandel
3 tablespoons honey
2 pounds fresh purple figs, stems removed
Whipping cream
Vanilla (optional)

Bring wine and honey to a boil. Add figs. Reduce heat and simmer fruit for 20 minutes. Cool figs in liquid and chill. Serves 6 to 8.
    Serve with plain, thick cream or whip with a dash of vanilla.

Zabaglione

Although traditionally prepared with Marsala wine, this frothy custard gives zabaglione a new twist.

6 egg whites
1/3 cup sugar
6 eggshell halves of Delicato White Port (1/2 cup)
Zest from one lemon

Beat egg yolks in top of double boiler over hot water. Gradually add sugar and port. Whisk continually until mixture thickens, increases in volume and is heated thoroughly. This may take as long as 10 minutes. Do not let mixture boil. Remove from heat. Reserve 1/2 cup of custard in separate container.
    Beat egg whites until stiff and fold into thickened custard. Spoon into 6 to 8 dishes. Drizzle reserved custard on top and sprinkle generously with lemon zest. This fragile concoction does not chill or keep. Serve immediately.

Variations: Without mixing with egg whites, you may use custard as a sauce to spoon over fresh fruit. Or present as a pudding, served in small portions.

Baked Apple Slices

This lightly sweet dish doubles as a side dish for roast pork, turkey or ham.

6 tart apples
Butter, as needed
3/4 cup Zinfandel
3/4 cup brown sugar
2 cinnamon sticks
Lemon rind of 1/2 lemon, grated
Nutmeg

Peel and core apples, trimming off tops and bottoms. Slice into 1/4-inch thick rings. Sauté gently in butter for 5 minutes. Arrange in baking dish and pour wine over them. Sprinkle on sugar. Place cinnamon sticks in wine and sprinkle on lemon rind and nutmeg. Bake at 325° until apples are soft (about 45 minutes). Serve hot as a dessert, with cream or ice cream, if you wish. Delicious hot or cold as a condiment. Serves 6.

Wine Suggestion: California port.

MAKE YOUR OWN ICE BLOCK

Create your own ice block to fit the occasion and the size of your bowl.
    Punches may be diluted slightly without changing their basic flavor and balance of liquids but should be watched carefully to detect too much dilution. When the ice block has melted considerably, and your party is still in full swing, remove the bowl to the kitchen area and replace the melted block with a fresh piece of ice.
    Decorative ice blocks must be watched carefully for melting, as the ice tends to break apart when too thin, spilling the decorations into the punch.

Striped Effect Block Ice

Take a half-gallon milk carton or ice cream carton and fill one-fourth full of water. Freeze. On top of ice, lay thinly sliced orange slices, cucumber slices, lemon rounds or other fruits or vegetables, overlapping slightly. Fill to one-half full. Freeze. Repeat procedure until you have a full block with three colorful layers.

Colored Ice Block

Create a striped effect by using colored water or fruit juices. Follow the procedure above.

Individual Ice Cubes

When serving punch from a pitcher, you may wish to place an individual ice cube into each cup or glass. For a decorative effect, put a long-stemmed cherry, a quarter-slice of lemon, or a pineapple cube into each ice cube tray before filling with water.

Baked Pears With Ginger

A simple preparation for an elegant dessert.

8 to 10 small, firm pears (Bosc pears work well)
1/2 cup sugar
1/2 teaspoon lemon rind
2 cups Zinfandel

Peel pears, leaving stems on. Preheat oven to 350°. Mix sugar, lemon rind and wine in shallow baking dish. Place pears upright in dish and bake about an hour, or until tender. Baste pears frequently.
Combine Ginger Cream ingredients and serve with warm or chilled pears. Serves 8 to 10.

GINGER CREAM:

1/2 pint heavy cream, whipped
1/4 cup powdered sugar
1 tablespoon (or more) finely grated fresh ginger

Fruit Compote

Ripe, fresh fruit gives the best results. Wonderful with hot, spiced tea.

1-1/2 cups crumbled coconut macaroons
1-1/2 cups sliced fresh plums
3 cups sliced and peeled peaches
1-1/2 cups halved strawberries
1/4 cup firmly packed brown sugar
1/2 cup Delicato Cream Sherry

Lightly butter a baking dish. Cover bottom with layer of macaroon crumbs. Add layer each of plums, peaches and berries. Alternate crumb and fruit layers, ending with crumbs. Sprinkle brown sugar and sherry on top. Bake 20 to 30 minutes at 350° or until fruit is fork-tender. Serve warm. Serves 8 (or 4 with second helpings).

PEACH WITH BURGUNDY

Pesca Con Vino Rosso

Fruit-flavored wine has been an Italian favorite for as long as people remember. The wine is drunk with the meal and the fruit eaten as a dessert. Apple, orange, plum and peach slices take this favorite through the seasons.
Place peeled fruit slices in a pitcher. Add a dry red wine, preferably a fruity Zinfandel. Let sit for an hour. Or, make a single serving by placing several fruit slices in a glass, then filling with wine.

1 large peach
2 ounces chilled California burgundy

Peel one large ripe peach and slice lengthwise. Place in large wine glass. Pour chilled wine over peach. Drink immediately. Makes one refreshing serving.

Crystallized Grapes

Serve several clusters in sherbet glasses as dessert, or use as a garnish for meat platters or fruit salads.

1 large cluster seedless green grapes (about 1 pound)
2 egg whites
1 tablespoon Delicato Green Hungarian
Finely granulated sugar

Divide cluster into bunches of approximately 8 to 10 grapes. Combine egg whites and wine, beating until blended, but not foamy. Dip grapes into egg white mixture and sprinkle with sugar. Place in single layer on attractive serving platter. Place in refrigerator until glazed and hardened. Serve cold.

Note: A combination of purple, red and green grapes is attractive interspersed with thin slices of summer melons. Serve with champagne or Chardonnay.

Peach Topping

Delicious over ice cream.

Joe Sciabica, Jr., grandson of founder, dipping apples into wine glass.

2 large peaches, peeled and sliced (about two cups)
1/4 cup sugar
1/2 cup Delicato Green Hungarian
3 whole allspice berries
Freshly grated nutmeg to taste

To peel whole peach, place in boiling water for 10 to 30 seconds, removing loosened skin and peach stone. Slice peach into 1/4-inch slices. Heat sugar and wine in saucepan over medium heat until sugar dissolves. Add allspice and nutmeg. Stir. Pour over peaches. Cover and refrigerate, stirring occasionally, until well chilled. Serve over vanilla, cinnamon or butterscotch ice cream. Serves 4.

Variation: Combine peaches and juice with other fruits for a fresh salad.

Dressings For Fruit

Last-minute assembly of ingredients makes a truly fresh fruit salad. White wine or citrus juice keeps the fruit from discoloring.

Strawberries—Store unwashed and uncovered in refrigerator. Hull and wash strawberries just before adding to salad.

Raspberries—To wash, place in colander and let water flow gently through them. Drain and shake lightly. Use berries at once.

Peaches—Peel fresh peaches by dropping in hot water for 10 seconds. Dip next in cold water and peel skin off in strips.

Melons—Refrigerate melons only long enough to chill, or delicate flavors will be lost. To form melon balls, cut melon in half horizontally, remove seeds and scoop out flesh with a small ball scoop.

Pears—Pears discolor and soften quickly so add to salad at the last minute.

Bananas—Slightly firm bananas are best in salads. Slice them just before serving to prevent discoloration.

Kiwi Fruit—Cut in half lengthwise and scoop out flesh with a spoon, or peel and slice thinly.

Apricots—Pit apricots by cutting in half with a knife, following the slight indentation. Twist the two halves in opposite directions to separate them and remove the pit.

I.

1/2 cup California dry sherry
1/4 cup honey
Juice of 1 lemon
Dash salt

Blend ingredients thoroughly and pour over your favorite tart fruits—apples, grapefruits, oranges, etc.

II.

This simple dressing is good over hulled and sliced strawberries, or served as a dip alongside unhulled strawberries.

1/2 cup sour cream
2 tablespoons Delicato Green Hungarian
1 tablespoon honey

III.

This creamy dressing is delicious on fruit salad. Try a combination of diced fresh pineapple, oranges, apples, adding tiny marshmallows for an old-fashioned taste.

1 package cream cheese (3 ounces)
1 tablespoon lemon juice
1 tablespoon sugar
1/4 cup California dry sherry
Dash salt

Soften cream cheese. Gradually add lemon juice and blend in remaining ingredients well.

Sweets

Spanish Basque Flan

SHERRIED COFFEE

Chilled or steaming, this drink finishes a good meal and a delightful evening.

8 cups strong, black coffee
1 cup light corn syrup
1 quart ice water
2 cups Delicato Cream Sherry
1 cup heavy cream, whipped

Combine coffee and corn syrup in saucepan, stirring continually. Bring to a boil and set aside. Pour coffee into a bowl. Blend in ice water and sherry.

Ladle from bowl or pour from pitcher. Top with a dollop of whipped cream. Serves 12 to 14, depending on size of cup.

Variation: If hot coffee is preferred, use boiling water and heated sherry. Serve immediately.

Delicato employee Joe Larrañaga shared this recipe with *Meet Delicato* readers in 1984. "It tastes just like the dish in my family's native country," Joe says.

3/4 cup sugar
6 eggs, well beaten
3/4 cup sugar
1 quart milk
1-1/2 teaspoons vanilla
1 tablespoon brandy (optional)
1/4 teaspoon salt
3 cinnamon sticks

Place 3/4 cup sugar in pan over medium heat. Shake pan until sugar begins to melt. Stir continually as syrup bubbles and turns from golden brown to rich brown. When syrup begins to caramelize on bottom of pan, check for thickness. Draw a "path" across bottom of pan with a wooden spoon. Consistency is right when syrup seeps slowly back, covering path. Remove immediately from heat and pour into heatproof bowl. Turn bowl around quickly so caramel coats sides evenly. (It looks like a lacquer coating inside the bowl.) Set aside.

Beat eggs until thick and lemon colored. Blend in sugar. Beat milk into sugar mixture. Add vanilla, brandy and salt. Strain through sieve into caramelized bowl. Place cinnamon sticks on top like hands of clock. Put bowl in shallow pan of hot water (a 9 x 13-inch cake pan works well). Bake in 325° oven for about 1 hour, or until knife inserted in center of flan comes out clean.

Chill overnight or at least 8 hours in refrigerator before inverting on plate to serve. Spoon caramelized syrup over each serving. Makes 10 persons happy once, but five persons twice. Tastes good the next day, if you should have any left.

Enjoy a cup of coffee and a glass of California cream sherry with this creamy dessert.

Belinda's Torte

A four-layer cake with a surprising snap of chocolate and a crunch of almonds. It was Belinda Cardoza's contribution to this year's family sausage making potluck supper.

1 package chocolate cake mix (2 layer size), or you can bake your own
8 ounces sweet chocolate
3/4 cup butter, room temperature
1/2 cup toasted almonds, coarsely chopped
2 cups whipped cream (or 8 ounces Cool Whip)

Bake cake in 2 lightly greased and floured 9-inch layer pans. Cool. Split each layer horizontally.

Melt 6 ounces of chocolate in double boiler over hot water. Cool slightly and beat in butter. Add almonds.

Spread one cake layer with half of chocolate mixture. Top with second layer and spread it with half of the whipped cream. Spread remaining chocolate on third layer and finish with whipped cream on top of the last layer.

Top with chocolate shavings made from remaining 2 ounces of chocolate. Refrigerate until serving. Serves 12 to 16.

Hint: For easier slicing, dip long-blade knife into glass of water before each cut. Wipe knife blade clean after slicing, and dip in water again.

At home, dessert was mainly home-made cakes or cookies. When we felt like something sweet we whipped up what we called the one-egg cake. We beat the batter by hand, for we never had an electric mixer, spiced it up with Raleigh's vanilla, baked it, and ate it without frosting.

Pancakes With Wine

The success of these tasty, light Yugoslavian pancakes arises from the carbonated mineral water and vigorous whisking.

2 large eggs
2 cups carbonated mineral or club soda water
2 teaspoons lemon rind
1/2 teaspoon salt
1 teaspoon vegetable oil
1-3/4 cups white flour
Oil for frying
Cherry or plum jam
Coarse white sugar
Wine Sauce

Place eggs and 1/2 cup mineral water in large bowl and whisk until frothy. Add lemon rind, salt and 1/4 cup water. Whisk. Add 1 teaspoon oil and 1/4 cup mineral water. Alternate remaining 1 cup water and flour, whisking vigorously until smooth and thinner than regular pancake batter.

Heat 8-inch skillet. Pour in oil, swirl until well coated and pour out. Pour 1/3 cup batter into hot skillet, swirling batter until it covers bottom of pan and is evenly distributed. After 30 seconds, turn pancake (or flip it!) and cook for an additional 1/2 minute. Place cooked pancake on platter. Repeat procedure, oiling pan before adding fresh batter. Stack cooked pancakes. Spread with jam immediately or wait until serving time. After spreading jam, fold pancake in half, then in half again, allowing 3 pancakes per serving. Sprinkle with sugar. Makes 12 pancakes.

WINE SAUCE:

1 cup Delicato Green Hungarian
3 large egg yolks
1/4 cup white sugar

In double boiler over hot water vigorously whisk wine, yolks and sugar until sauce begins to thicken. Serve hot over pancakes.

Portuguese Doughnuts

Filozes

Filozes are deeper in color than American doughnuts. The irregular shapes resemble brown leaves with upturned edges.

1-1/2 cups milk, lukewarm (105°-115°)
1/2 cup warm water
1/2 cup sugar
2 teaspoons salt
2 packages dry yeast (1/4 ounce each)
2 eggs, room temperature, slightly beaten
1/2 cup soft margarine or shortening
7 to 7-1/2 cups sifted flour
1/4 cup milk
Oil for frying
Granulated sugar or white corn syrup

Making Portuguese donuts. Three generations, Dorothy Indelicato, Mary Cardoza and Marie Indelicato, 1985.

Add yeast to warm water, stirring until completely dissolved. Set aside. Mix milk, sugar and salt and combine with yeast mixture. Add eggs and margarine or shortening. Add flour in 2 additions, kneading mixture until dough is easy to handle and does not stick to hands. Place in lightly greased bowl and turn once so entire dough ball is greased. Let rise until double. Punch down and let rise a second time.

Dip fingers in small bowl of milk, then pinch off about 2 tablespoons of dough. Holding dough in both hands, use fingertips and thumbs to stretch dough into a 4-inch circle. Avoid thick edges by stretching until circle is thin throughout. Don't worry about small tears. Holding dough in hands, poke hole in center of circle from underneath with middle finger. Keep hands wet with milk while forming doughnuts.

Carefully place in 2 inches of hot shortening. Brown doughnuts on one side, about 2 minutes. Using tongs, flip over to other side and fry until brown. Remove to drain on absorbent paper. While hot, sprinkle with granulated sugar or drizzle with corn syrup. Eat the same day or freeze after baking. Makes 4 dozen.

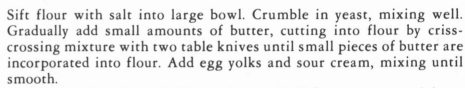

Koláčky

Kathy Szul, a computer operator at Delicato Vineyards, shares a recipe from her husband's family. "When I married into the Szul family, my husband's relatives came to visit and cook with me. They were eager to share their family Polish recipes with me."

4 cups flour
1/2 teaspoon salt
1 cake yeast (1 ounce)
3/4 pound butter
6 egg yolks
1/2 pint sour cream

Tom Strong, Jr., grandson of man who brought in our first six steel tanks.

Sift flour with salt into large bowl. Crumble in yeast, mixing well. Gradually add small amounts of butter, cutting into flour by criss-crossing mixture with two table knives until small pieces of butter are incorporated into flour. Add egg yolks and sour cream, mixing until smooth.

Gather dough into ball, turning until all flour is removed from bottom of bowl. Place in refrigerator overnight.

Lightly flour and sugar board or cloth for rolling dough. Cut dough ball into 4 pieces. Roll each piece into rectangle or square 1/4 inch thick. (Squares can be as large as 4 inches. Allow proportionately more filling per pastry and a few additional minutes baking time for larger cookies.) Roll each square again for additional thinness.

Place 1 teaspoon walnut or poppyseed filling on one corner of square. Roll up lightly to opposite corner. Place pastry seam-side down on ungreased baking sheet, 1/2 inch apart. Bake at 325° 20 to 25 minutes, until lightly brown. Let cool and remove to plate. Sift powdered sugar lightly on top.

Recipe makes approximately 8 dozen cookies.

WALNUT FILLING:

3 cups ground walnuts
1-1/2 cups sugar
1 tablespoon lemon juice
Lukewarm water

Combine walnuts and sugar. Stir in lemon juice and enough water to make moist but firm (about 4 tablespoons). Makes enough for one recipe.

Cheese Blintzes

Marilynne Davis, Marketing Services Secretary, recalls fond childhood memories of her mother making blintzes. "I ate them warm or hot, and any time of the day," she says.

6 eggs
1-1/2 teaspoons salt
1-1/2 cups flour
1-1/2 cups milk
Butter and oil for frying

Beat eggs until frothy. Add salt and flour, stirring to make a smooth paste. Add milk, stirring constantly.

Heat about 2 teaspoons vegetable oil and about 1/2 teaspoon butter in 6-inch crepe pan or skillet. Tilt pan in all directions to coat it completely. When grease is quite hot, pour about 3 tablespoons batter into skillet and tilt immediately in all directions to cover the bottom of the pan with a thin layer of batter.

When batter is set on top (no liquid spots left) and lightly browned on bottom, turn blintze out of pan, uncooked side down, onto a kitchen towel. Stir batter frequently and continue until all batter is used. Add oil and butter to the skillet when needed, while keeping a moderately hot temperature. Fill blintzes when all are fried on one side.

CHEESE FILLING:

1 pound small curd cottage cheese
8 ounces cream cheese
1 tablespoon softened butter
2 eggs
1/2 teaspoon salt
1 tablespoon sugar
Butter for frying
Sour cream

Beat cheeses and soft butter together. Add eggs, salt and sugar. Mix well. Place 1 heaping tablespoon in the middle of each blintze, on fried side. Fold like an envelope, raising bottom flap to cover filling, then bringing top flap down. Finally, fold both ends in to meet in center.* Place seam side down in a skillet with about 3 tablespoons sizzling butter and fry on both sides until golden brown. Serve hot with dollop of sour cream. Makes a dozen blintzes.

Blintzes may be frozen at this point. Wrap each one in foil and place in freezer until solid. Then pack in a heavy plastic bag. Remove from freezer as you need them. Either bake on a greased cookie sheet at 375° for about 20 minutes, or fry in butter until golden brown and heated through.

AFTER-SKI WARMTH

1 orange
6 to 8 whole cloves
3 cinnamon sticks
2 bottles California
   burgundy or Zinfandel (750 ml)
1/2 cup sugar

Stud orange with cloves. Set aside.
   Mix wine with sugar in crock pot. Add orange and cinnamon sticks. Simmer covered until hot. Serve directly from crock pot into punch cups. Makes 12 four-ounce servings— usually enough to last four people through a long evening of sipping.

Chocolate Mousse

You will make this easy, rich dessert often. It finishes good meals with a flourish.

6 ounces semisweet chocolate
5 eggs, separated
1 teaspoon vanilla
2 teaspoons brewed coffee
1 cup heavy cream
3 tablespoons Delicato White Port
1/4 cup sugar
Chocolate shavings

Melt chocolate in double boiler. Beat egg yolks to lemon color and gradually stir into chocolate. Add vanilla and coffee. Remove from heat.

In mixing bowl, beat cream until thick. Stir in port and fold mixture into chocolate. In another bowl, beat egg whites and sugar until stiff. Carefully fold into chocolate mixture. Pour into large bowl or individual dessert dishes. Top with chocolate shavings. Chill for at least 2 hours. Cover tightly with plastic wrap so crust will not form on top of mousse. Serves 6 to 8.

TOP HAT

3/4 cup Delicato Burgundy
1/3 cup orange juice
1 tablespoon powdered sugar
Ice cubes
1 tablespoon Delicato Port
Fresh fruit

Stir burgundy, orange juice and sugar in a tall glass until sugar dissolves. Add ice cubes. Float port on top. Garnish with fruit. Makes a single serving.

Wine Plum Ice

4 cups California burgundy (a 750 ml bottle)
2 cups water
3/4 cup sugar
2 tablespoons grated lemon peel
1 cinnamon stick
2 tablespoons lemon juice

Combine wine, water, sugar, lemon peel and cinnamon stick in saucepan. Bring to a boil, stirring often, until sugar dissolves. Reduce heat and simmer 5 minutes, uncovered.

Cool mixture to room temperature. Add lemon juice and remove cinnamon stick. Pour mixture in shallow pans (9 x 13-inch cake pans work well) and freeze overnight or for several days.

Several hours before serving, blend half mixture in blender or food processor until smooth. Repeat procedure with second half. Return mixture to pan and refreeze. Fifteen minutes before serving, transfer ice to refrigerator to soften.

Spoon into individual bowls. Garnish with fresh fruits such as orange, melon, pear or peach slices, or serve simply with mint garnish. Serves 8 to 10, depending on size of portions.

Cranberry Apple Pie

Cranberries give a rosy hue to this autumn dessert.

Pie pastry for 2-crust, 9-inch pie
5 cups sliced, peeled apples
1-1/2 cups fresh, uncooked cranberries
1 cup sugar
3 tablespoons flour
1/2 teaspoon cinnamon
Dash salt
1 teaspoon butter
1 teaspoon sugar and 1/4 teaspoon cinnamon, mixed
Whipped cream (optional)
2 tablespoons Delicato White Port

Preheat oven to 400°. Place bottom crust in pie plate and refrigerate while making filling.

Combine apples, cranberries, sugar, flour, cinnamon and salt. Toss lightly. Spoon mixture into chilled pie crust. Add dabs of butter. Roll out second crust, slitting top for vents. Place over fruit. Sprinkle with mixture of cinnamon and sugar.

Bake 40 minutes at 400°. Serve pie at room temperature with whipped cream or with thin slices of Colby or Mild Cheddar cheese. Serves 8.

Pumpkin Squares

2 cups sugar
4 eggs
1 cup salad oil
1 can pumpkin (29 ounces)
3-1/2 cups sifted flour
3 teaspoons cinnamon
1-1/4 teaspoons salt
2 teaspoons baking soda
2 tablespoons California medium sherry
1-1/2 cups chopped walnuts
3/4 cup raisins

Mary Indelicato.

Mix sugar and eggs. Add oil and pumpkin. Sift flour with cinnamon, salt and baking soda. Add to pumpkin mixture. Stir in sherry. Add nuts and raisins.

Pour into lightly greased 14 x 20-inch pan. Bake 35 to 40 minutes at 350°. This dessert keeps well refrigerated for several days or can be frozen. Serve plain or with whipped cream. Makes 24 squares.

Anise Cookies

Now, fifty years after the winery's founding we have a 30 million gallon facility—almost ten thousand times larger than the first vintage of just over three thousand gallons.

Through all these changes and growth, though, we have never lost sight of the fact that this winery is the realization of the dream of our Dad—a young Italian immigrant who came to this country seeking a good life.

This is a favorite Indelicato family recipe.

1 cup sugar
1/2 cup butter or margarine (1 cube)
1 tablespoon anise seeds, crushed
3 eggs
3 cups flour
3 teaspoons baking powder
1/2 teaspoon salt
Milk
Sesame seeds (optional)

Mix sugar with butter and anise seeds. Beat in eggs. Sift flour, baking powder, and salt together and add to mixture.

On lightly floured surface shape dough with hands into loaves 2 inches wide x 1/2 inch thick x length of cookie sheet. Lightly flatten with fingers. Brush with milk and sprinkle with sesame seeds, if desired. Bake at 350° for 20 minutes, or until golden.

Remove from oven. Immediately cut into 1/2 to 3/4-inch diagonal slices. Return to oven and bake for an additional 15 minutes until lightly toasted. Makes about 48 cookies. Traditionally served at the Indelicato home with their own Green Hungarian wine.

The Indelicatos, Anthony, Vincent, and Frank.

INDEX

The Wine Appreciation Guild Books
"The Classic Series on Cooking With Wine"

This series of ten wine cookbooks is the largest collection of cooking with wine recipes available in the World. There is no duplication of features or recipes in the Wine Advisory Board Cookbooks. Specific wine types are recommended as table beverages for all main dishes. The present series represents over 3,000 different recipes of all types using wine. From wine cocktails, hors d'oeuvres, salads, soups, wild game, fish, eggs, many different main dishes to desserts and jellies; the magnitude of this collection of wine recipes is overwhelming. Who could possibly develop and test such a large number of recipes? These books are the result of the cooperation of over 400 people in the wine industry. In 1961 the Wine Advisory Board began collecting the favorite and best recipes of various winemakers and their families. Most of the recipes are old family favorites, tested with time and then re-tested and proven in Wine Advisory Board test kitchens. We are particularly pleased with the recipes and wine choices from staff members of the Department of Viticulture and Enology and the Department of Food Science and Technology of University of California, Davis and Fresno.

So here is a series of the very best wine recipes; selected and developed by many of the most knowledgeable wine and food lovers of America.

#500 EPICUREAN RECIPES OF CALIFORNIA WINE-MAKERS: Did you know that you can buy wild boar, cook it at home with Burgundy and produce a gourmet treat that your guests will rave about for years? Or, that you can make your reputation as an Epicurean cook by preparing and serving Boeuf a la Bourguinonne, according to the recipe of a famous wine authority? This book includes the most elaborate to simple recipes contributed by California Winemakers, their wives and associates; all selected for their unforgettable taste experiences. Another important feature of this book is the comprehensive index of recipes for the entire six cookbook series, 128 pp, 8½" x 11", illustrated, 1984 edition. $6.95 @ ISBN 0-932664-00-8.

#501 GOURMET WINE COOKING THE EASY WAY: All new recipes for memorable eating, prepared quickly and simply with wine. Most of the recipes specify convenience foods which can be delightfully flavored with wine, enabling the busy homemaker to set a gourmet table for family and friends with a minimum of time in the kitchen. More than 500 tested and proven recipes; used frequently by the first families of America's wine industry. 128 pp, 8½" x 11", illustrated, 1980 edition. $6.95 @ ISBN 0-932664-01-6.

#502 NEW ADVENTURES IN WINE COOKERY BY CALIFORNIA WINEMAKERS: New Revised 1984 Edition, includes many new recipes from California's new winemakers. The life work of the winemaker is to guide nature in the development in wine of beauty, aroma, bouquet and subtle flavors. Wine is part of their daily diet, leading to more flavorful dishes, comfortable living, merriment and goodfellowship. These recipes contributed by Winemakers, their families and colleagues represent this spirit of flavorful good living. A best selling cookbook with 500 exciting recipes including barbecue, wine drinks, salads and sauces. 128 pp, illustrated, 8½" x 11", $6.95 @ ISBN 0-932664-10-5.

#503 FAVORITE RECIPES OF CALIFORNIA WINE-MAKERS: The original winemakers' cookbook and a bestseller for fifteen years. Over 200 dedicated winemakers, their wives and colleagues have shared with us their love of cooking. They are the authors of this book, which is dedicated to a simple truth known for thousands of years in countless countries: good food is even better with wine. Over 500 authentic recipes, many used for generations, are included in this "cookbook classic". Revised Edition 1981. 128 pp, 8½" x 11", illustrated, $6.95 @ ISBN 0-932664-03-2.

#504 DINNER MENUS WITH WINE By Emily Chase and Wine Advisory Board. Over 100 complete dinner menus with recommended complimentary wines. This book will make your dinner planning easy and the results impressive to your family and most sophisticated guests. Emily Chase worked with the winemakers of California a number of years and was also the Home Economics Editor of Sunset Magazine. She tested recipes for six years and is the author of numerous articles and books on cooking. This edition contains 400 different recipes, suggestions for wines to accompany dinners and tips on serving, storing and enjoying wine. 1981 Edition, 128 pp, illustrated, 8½" x 11", $6.95 @ ISBN 0-932664-30-X.

#505 EASY RECIPES OF CALIFORNIA WINEMAK-ERS: "I wonder often what vintners buy one-half so precious as the stuff they sell" questioned Omar Khayyam 1100 A.D. We wonder what the vintners could possibly eat one-half so delicious as the food they prepare. This is a collection of "precious" recipes that are easy to prepare and each includes the vintner's favorite beverage. Many are recipes concocted in the vintner's kitchens and some are family favorites proven for their flavor and ease of preparation. No duplication with the other cookbooks. 128 pp, illustrated, 8½" x 11", $6.95 @ ISBN 0-932664-05-9.

#855 POCKET ENCYCLOPEDIA OF AMERICAN WINE, EAST OF THE ROCKIES by Wm. Kaufman. Companion to the author's best-selling POCKET ENCYCLOPEDIA OF CALIFORNIA WINE and other Western states. A convenient and thorough reference listing all Eastern American wineries with vital information on vineyards, winemaking practices, climate, viticulture, appellations, tasting terms, visiting information and maps. Wineries from Texas and Colorado, through the Midwest, the South, to New York and New England included. Also tasting notes and award winning wines. 144 pp, 7½" x 3½", gold imprinted leatherette cover. $5.95 @ ISBN 0-932664-41-5. 1985 Edition.

#554 WINE CELLAR RECORD BOOK: A professionally planned, elegant, leatherette bound cellar book for the serious wine collector. Organized by the wine regions of the World, helpful for keeping perpetual inventories and monitoring the aging of each wine in your cellar. Enough space for over 200 cases of wine and space to record tasting notes and special events. Illustrated, 12" x 10½", six ring binder, additional pages available. $32.50 @ ISBN 0-932664-06-7.

#640 THE CHAMPAGNE COOKBOOK: "Add Some Sparkle to Your Cooking and Your Life" by Malcolm R. Hébert. Cooking with Champagne is a glamorous yet easy way to liven up your cuisine. The recipes range from soup, salads, hors d'oeuvres, fish, fowl, red meat, vegetables and of course desserts—all using Champagne. Many new entertaining ideas with Champagne cocktails, drinks and Champagne lore are included along with simple rules on cooking with and serving Sparkling Wines. Recipes are provided by California, New York and European Champagne makers and their families. The author's 30 years of teaching and writing about food and wine makes this an elegant yet practical book. 128 pp, illustrated, 8½" x 11", ppb, $6.95 @ ISBN 0-932664-07-5.

#641 THE POCKET ENCYCLOPEDIA OF CALIFORNIA WINE and OTHER WESTERN STATES: "The most useful little book on California wine yet." A convenient and thorough reference book that fits in vest pocket. provides answers to most questions about California wines, the wineries, grape varieties and wine terms. Includes maps and a tasting note section. Handy to carry with you to restaurants, wine tastings and wine shops to make intelligent selections. Display Box Billboard Available. Covers Northwestern, Southwestern States and Mexico. 336 pp, 7¾" x 3½", $5.95 @ ISBN 0-932664-40-7. 1985-86 Edition.

#672 WINE IN EVERYDAY COOKING by Patti Ballard. Patti is the popular wine consultant from Santa Cruz who has been impressing winery visitors and guests for years with her wine recipes and the cooking tips from Patti's grandmother. Chapters range from soup and hors d'oeuvres through pasta, fish and desserts—all of course using wine. 128 pp, illustrated, 8½" x 11", ppb, $5.95 @ ISBN 0-932664-20-2.

#727 WINE LOVERS COOKBOOK by Malcolm Hébert. The newest and most unique in our Wine Cookbook Series with 100 winning recipes from the National Cooking With Wine Contest. All recipes have been tested and written for easy preparation and reliable results. They range from Artichoke Appetizer with wine to Cold Apricot Soup, Limehouse Chicken to Pumpkin Beef Stew. And in-depth chapter on California wine, a wine & food chart and cooking with wine tips are included. With a bottle of wine at hand and this book, you too will be a winner in the kitchen. 176 pp, illustrated, 8½" x 11", $7.95 @ ISBN 0-932664-29-6.

#673 THE CALIFORNIA WINE DRINK BOOK by William I. Kaufman. Cocktails, hot drinks, punches and coolers all made with wine. Over 200 different drink recipes, using various wines along with mixing tips and wine entertaining suggestions. Today's accent on lighter drinks makes this a most useful handbook, and you'll save money too by using wine rather than higher taxed liquors! Pocket size, leatherette cover, 128 pp, $4.95. May 1982, ISBN 0-932664-10-9.

#914 WINE, FOOD & THE GOOD LIFE by Arlene Mueller & Dorothy Indelicato. "Celebrating 50 years of family winemaking." Here is a cookbook with generation-proven, wine family recipes complimented by contemporary California cuisine recipes, and wine entertaining tips. The California Wine Country lifestyle is captured through fascinating historical anecdotes from three generations of winemaking, old photos and lots of sharing of cooking tips from the winemakers and their wives. Recipes range from quick and easy to "gourmet" and represent a variety of ethnic backgrounds with Italian predominating. 144 pp, illustrated, 8½" x 11", $7.95 @ ISBN 0-932664-47-4. 1985

HOW TO ORDER BY MAIL: Indicate the number of copies and titles you wish on the order form below and include your check, money order, or Mastercard, or VISA card number. California residents include 6½% sales tax. There is a $3.00 shipping and handling charge per order, regardless of how many books you order. (If no order form—any paper will do.)

ORDER FORM
WINE APPRECIATION GUILD
155 Connecticut Avenue
San Francisco, California 94104

SHIP TO: _____

Address _____

City _____ State _____ Zip _____

Please send the following:

_____ Copies #500 EPICUREAN RECIPES OF CALIFORNIA WINEMAKERS	$6.95@	_____
_____ Copies #501 GOURMET WINE COOKING THE EASY WAY	$6.95@	_____
_____ Copies #502 NEW ADVENTURES IN WINE COOKERY	$6.95@	_____
_____ Copies #503 FAVORITE RECIPES OF CALIFORNIA WINEMAKERS	$6.95@	_____
_____ Copies #504 DINNER MENUS WITH WINE	$6.95@	_____
_____ Copies #505 EASY RECIPES OF CALIFORNIA WINEMAKERS	$6.95@	_____
_____ Copies #554 WINE CELLAR RECORD BOOK	$32.50@	_____
_____ Copies #640 THE CHAMPAGNE COOKBOOK	$6.95@	_____
_____ Copies #641 POCKET ENCYCLOPEDIA OF CALIFORNIA WINES	$5.95@	_____
_____ Copies #672 CALIFORNIA WINE DRINK BOOK	$4.95@	_____
_____ Copies #673 WINE IN EVERYDAY COOKING	$5.95@	_____
_____ Copies #727 WINE LOVERS' COOKBOOK	$7.95@	_____
_____ Copies #855 POCKET ENCYCLOPEDIA OF AMERICAN WINES EAST OF THE ROCKIES	$5.95@	_____
_____ Copies #914 WINE, FOOD AND THE GOOD LIFE	$7.95@	_____
	Subtotal	_____
California Residents 6½% sales tax		_____
plus $3.00 Shipping and handling (per order)		$3.00
TOTAL enclosed or charged to credit card		_____

_____ Please charge to my Mastercard or Visa card # _____

Expiration Date _____

Signature _____